Perspectives in English Book One

Ray Beecroft & Graham Sanderson

Hart-Davis Educational

© 1982 Ray Beecroft and Graham Sanderson

ISBN 0 247 13163 6

Published by Hart-Davis Educational Ltd
a division of Granada Publishing
Frogmore, St Albans, Hertfordshire

Granada ®
Granada Publishing ®

Filmset and printed in Great Britain by
BAS Printers Limited, Over Wallop, Hampshire

Design and cover design: Ken Vail Graphic Design

Drawings

John Holder *pages* 27, 98, 125

Robert Geary *pages* 55, 56, 61, 105, 115, 116, 122, 132, 139

Barry Wilkinson *pages* 7, 8, 10, 14, 15, 19, 32, 33, 85, 90, 99, 111,
    136, 140, 164, 165, 166, 167.

To the Teacher

This book in the series aims to provide stimulating material appropriate to the ages and abilities of eleven to twelve-year-olds in a comprehensive school.

Nine of the chapters in Book One are based on themes and contain material for discussion, comprehension and writing. There are also two Language chapters and a list of spelling groups. In addition, each thematic chapter is supplemented by a *Starting Point*, not related to the theme.

The thematic chapters are based on the assumption that much classroom work will involve discussion as well as writing. Questions and assignments in the text are identified by asterisks or by numbers. An asterisk denotes a question intended primarily for discussion; a numbered question usually demands a written response. These marks are for the teacher's convenience and are not intended to be prescriptive.

Specific language instruction in the book is grouped separately from the thematic chapters for ease of reference. A short index to language topics covered here and elsewhere in the book is given on page 173.

The *Starting Points* offer stimulus for imaginative work; or attempt to teach a skill; or deal with a particular aspect of language.

G.S.
C.R.B.

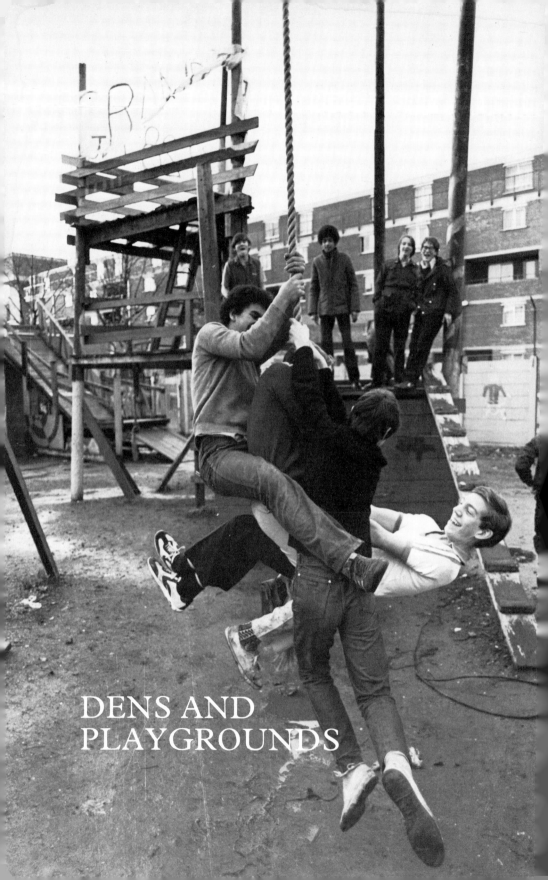

DENS AND
PLAYGROUNDS

Dens

Here is a description, written by an eleven year old girl, of a den which she made with the help of her sister and a friend.

A few years ago we made a den. There is an old lane which runs down our avenue at the back of the houses. We live at the end of the avenue so we have the big corner piece at the bottom of our garden.

Alison, Ann and I built our den in this corner. We got planks of wood for the walls, and a piece of corrugated iron for the roof. Alison made some curtains for the windows. These were made from old bits of material, and put on a piece of string along the top of the window. The windows were made from transparent plastic, fastened to the wall with nails. The door was an old garage door which my dad had just taken off our garage.

Inside our den we made some seats. There was a bench. This was made from a plank of wood resting on two smaller pieces of wood which were hammered into the ground. There was also a chair. This was an old deck-chair which was going to be thrown out because the seat was broken. We found another seat and put the chair in our den. My dad made us a table out of old scraps of wood. The den was now finished and we spent a lot of time in it. Once we even had our tea in it.

A cross section and plan of the den on page 7

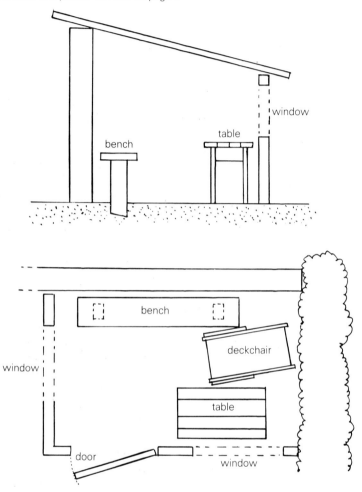

* Have you ever built or used a den?

* What sorts of places do you think are best for building dens?

* What materials can be used for building dens?

* Have you ever had a den that was destroyed by other people?

* Have you ever built or used a den that was really secret, known only to you or a few of your friends?

1. Describe a den you have built or used. Explain how you built or found it, what you put in it and what happened there. Illustrate your writing with labelled drawings.

The Cave

In this extract, Ginger and his three friends, Tiny, Andy and Toni, build a den out of a cave which they find in a canal bank.

Ginger had marked the spot in his mind, as well as he could, but it was nearly dinner-time before they found it. It was near the old woman's house, where they hadn't liked to play. It had an elder bush directly in front of it. If it hadn't been for that beam of sun shining through the leaves straight into the cave, Ginger would never have seen it. At one time there had been a tree on this spot, but it must have fallen away from the road and been cut off close. In falling, the tree had dragged the roots out of the ground, and they had come upwards with a ton of clay and pebbles caught between them. The space under the roots was deep and wide. It was a perfect hiding place.

One by one they crawled through the elder bush into the cave. It ran back at least eight feet into the bank, and they could sit upright without bending their necks.

'It's d-dry,' said Andy, smoothing the baked wall.

'It's safe,' said Tiny, peering out through the thick screen of leaves.

'It's OK,' said Ginger, trying to keep his voice ordinary. 'It's OK.'

The days that followed were the best they'd ever had. Every morning they sneaked along the canal bank without meeting the canal man. Saturdays and Sundays they had to look out for Bert Hughes. Every day they had to be back in their street before six, when he and his lot came home from work. If he'd seen the gang all returning together every evening he'd soon have been on their trail.

There was a lot to do. First there were sacks to find, the old ones being burned in the fire. Andy's father got some from the shop where he worked – although they didn't tell him what they wanted them for – and they carried them stuffed down inside their shirts where they tickled horribly. They put the sacks on the floor. Then Mr Reynolds gave Toni some wooden boxes that his potatoes came in. They took them to pieces, stuck the pieces down their trousers and knocked them together inside the cave with Ginger's dad's hammer. Afterwards they had to pick the splinters out of one another's behinds. These boxes were their seats. If they had anything to eat they ate it off their knees.

There were ridges in the walls which they used as shelves. Here they kept nails and string and two night-lights that Tiny had begged from his married sister. When they were lit they looked like stars. They found a couple of tiles that had blown off the grocer's roof, and with these they scraped further into the bank, until they'd made a space big enough for a boy to lie down in.

As the days went by they got more ambitious. They fetched wrappings from Petty Market to stuff the sacks, cramming the paper inside their shirts so that they looked like girls. They hung round the pub in the evening and collected the crisps left in the bottoms of the packets. They stored these in a tin they got from Bill Klein, trading it for two foreign stamps and four of Rene's empty nail varnish bottles. They had two lemonade bottles for water but they couldn't find anywhere to fill them. They couldn't drink canal water.

from *Ginger over the Wall* by Prudence Andrew

∗ Why does Ginger have to keep his voice **ordinary** when he describes the den as 'OK'?

∗ Why is the cave so suitable as a site for a den?

∗ Why do the boys go to such great pains to hide what they are doing from anyone else, particularly the '**canal man**' and Bert Hughes and 'his lot'?

∗ How can you tell that Bert Hughes and his gang are older and bigger than Ginger and his friends?

∗ The boys work very hard to improve the cave, but it does not sound as though they think of their efforts as 'work': why not?

1. Draw a plan and a cross-section of the cave, showing how it is formed and what the boys have put in it.

Playgrounds

In cities where children have little room to play, some councils set up adventure playgrounds for children, where they can lark about, build things and enjoy themselves under the care of a leader. Perhaps you are a member of such a playground.

In her book, Workyards, *Nancy Rudolph (who is American) describes such a playground.*

Workyards are more than playgrounds. They are places where children play in any way they elect. Limitations are set by the space that is available and the always changing and abundant supply of materials: lumber, nails, tools, old machinery, rope, sinks, stoves, pickets from an old fence, barrels and planks. These are places where children can play as they will: they can be noisy or wild, or quiet and contemplative. Children will arrive with the crudest building skills and learn by experimentation, by trial and error, and through success how to achieve a goal. A playleader is always there to show how things can be done (and not what *should* be done). The child is architect, designer, inventor, builder. He does the planning and the changing. Enthusiasm may be sporadic; a project worked on for days may be abandoned temporarily, but in a Workyard that project is there when the builder returns re-enthused to continue or ready to start something new. The Workyard is his kingdom and the community protects his right to it.

In a Workyard children have a chance to exert themselves to achieve an objective. In a word, they work. Freedom and space exist for a number of choices and a variety of activities. There is music and dancing, gardening, caring for animals, ball games, exercising, painting and drawing. There is room for physical challenge: children can clamber up ropes and burrow through tunnels, and if they are lucky there is space for ball games and acrobatics. Corners and crannies can be found in which to build camp fires for roasting potatoes. Old bedsteads and mattresses can be arranged to make a hospital or a furniture store. Cast-off bits and pieces become barter at a trading post. One of the most compelling activities is constructing. Supplied with wood and tools children become builders of huts, dens, houses, barns, stables, lean-tos, hideaways – an assortment of constructions to defy adult imagination. In a Workyard children achieve their own order in their own style.

from *Workyards* by Nancy Rudolph

* Nancy Rudolph insists on calling these places **Workyards** and says, of the children who go there: 'In a word, they work.' How is it that different people can call the same place a **playground** and a **workyard**? When does work become play, and play become work?

* What does Nancy Rudolph mean when she says, '**Limitations are set by the space available.**'?

* What does **contemplative** mean?

* What does **through trial and error** mean?

* What does **goal** mean, in this case?

* What does **sporadic** mean?

* What are the differences between a hut, a house and a lean-to; a barn and a stable; a den and a hideaway?

Suppose you live in a city where the council have been knocking down some big, old houses in order to build new ones. They decide to leave an area for local children to use as an adventure playground, with a paid, full-time leader. Part of this area was previously covered by two old houses, and the rest by their gardens. Some of the outhouses of the old buildings have been left standing. They are bare of furniture, but can be locked and have electricity and water supplied to them. The council have built a high fence round the site with two lockable gates. Here is a plan of the site:

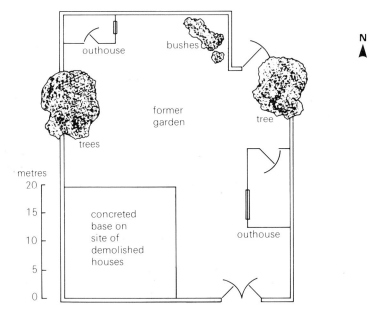

Suppose that the council decide to ask the people most concerned (that is, the local children) to submit plans, showing how they would lay out the site as an adventure playground. The council require ideas in the form of a plan and a written report. You are one of the children asked.

1. Make a list of the ten things that you would most like to include in the playground, in any order. Remember that there will be very little money available, so do not include expensive items.

When you have made your list, look at the list below and see if there are any items or ideas here which you would like to include.

Re-write your list in order of importance, including some of these items if you wish.

An 'adventure' area
   (for building, climbing, tunnelling, bonfires, etc.)
An area for ball games
A pet-house (for guinea-pigs, rabbits, pigeons, etc.)
A safe area for under-fives
A sand-pit
A pond
A garden for planting vegetables and flowers
A games or activities area
A leader's room
A lockable store for tools
A 'tidy' area for storing materials

2. Draw a plan showing how you would fit the various items you have chosen into the site.

In addition, write a letter to the local council explaining your reasons for planning the site in the way you have done. Your letter might begin like this:

Dear Sir,
          Here is my plan for the new adventure playground. I have made a list below of the items which I think ought to be included in the playground and my reasons for suggesting them.
     One . . .

3. When all the plans and reports are completed, organise yourselves into groups of three or four. Each group should look at and consider as many plans and reports as possible produced by others in the class, and select the one they like best. In considering the plans, each group should bear the following points in mind:

a. There is little money to spend on this project, so costly ideas might have to be rejected.

b. If you like a plan very much but dislike one or two items or feel that some things are too costly, you may decide to accept the plan on the condition that those items are cut out or changed.

c. If you are impressed by a particular plan and letter, make a note of its author's name and a note of any changes you would make in the plan before passing it on to another group.

d. At the end of your discussions, you may be expected to explain to the rest of the class which plan you have chosen, and why.

* By touring wastegrounds, and asking in shops and workplaces in the area, you have managed to collect the following items which might be useful in the playground:

bricks
breeze blocks
planks (several; assorted lengths from one to four metres)
rough timber (some logs: up to 50 centimetres wide, and some old floorboards and fence posts)
small pieces of wood (off-cuts from a timber yard)
ropes
old car tyres
sacks
string
large sheets of paper (mostly wrapping paper)
cardboard
boxes (mostly cardboard, of all sizes, and wooden fruit boxes)
expanded polystyrene foam in small blocks
two old doors
some plastic guttering and drain-pipe sections
poles (mostly old broom-handles)
lots of pieces of wire
tiles (some broken)
some old pieces of carpet
pieces of canvas
bicycle parts (including wheels)

How might you use these materials? Would you reject any of these things and not use them? Are there things which you think would be very useful but which are not on the list? What would you use such things for? How would you go about finding them? Would you restrict the use of any of the materials, to older children only, for example?

4. Suppose that the local council have now received the plans and reports you sent to them and have agreed, in principle, that the playground should be opened in due course. However, some people who live near the site object on the grounds that it will be noisy and untidy. Several of these people write letters to the local newspaper.

Write one of these letters yourself, protesting about the proposed playground.

Or: Write a letter to the Editor of the newspaper, defending the playground.

Bennie's and Maxine's Playground

Here is a conversation between two children, Bennie and Maxine which was recorded as they walked around their adventure playground.

Maxine : There's lots of swings over there and you can climb up this one and go across the bridge to that one.

Bennie : They've got a rope going from that tower to the swing over there and you have to go right the way across and you're hanging and if you drop it's your hard luck. It's about as high as one of those telegraph poles. I go across it – I don't go like monkeys, you know, I keep on the top: I put that foot over there and lay down on it and pull myself along. You get a lot of blisters up here! I like it in winter best because they all have snow fights. There was a man kept on hitting us with snowballs, so we all lined up, got a load of dustbin lids and started fighting him, got it all in the eyes and everything. See that shed over there? There was a lot of tame rats in it, but they all got out.

Maxine : I saw one of Tommy's rats over there one day.

Bennie : There was a lot of huts but they burnt them all out. They normally make huts every year, every summer. They had a little car built of wood last year, didn't they? Put tyres all round it.

Maxine : The little ones used to get bags full of clothes and make out they was going on their holidays.

Bennie : There's a football pitch over there.

Maxine : The girls play games over there sometimes. Here, that tower, the one you can see through, that's been here for years now.

Bennie : It's made out of sleepers.

Maxine : See where there's a ladder over there? Sometimes we get up there and we sit up there and we talk about the stars and all that.

Bennie : You wouldn't think you could see a thing over a thousand miles away, would you?

from *Adventure Playgrounds* by Jack Lamberts

* How can you tell that Bennie and Maxine are proud of their playground?

* What activities do they mention that go on in the playground?

* Quote lines which show that Bennie and Maxine are talking to someone else, not just to one another.

* Quote some lines which show that this is spoken language, not written. How can you be sure?

* Compare Nancy Rudolph's description (on page 11) of the activities that go on in a 'Workyard' with Bennie and Maxine's description of what they do in their playground. What differences do you notice in the way their thoughts are expressed?

1. Imagine you are showing someone — perhaps a schoolfriend who is new to the area — the places where you play. Write down the conversation just as it might be spoken. You might find it useful to improvise the conversation first with a friend in the classroom.

2. Suppose your local council is threatening to build houses or shops on some of the places where you play. Write down what you might say at a meeting with an official from the council explaining where you play and what you do, so that he or she understands why you want to be able to continue using the area as a playground.

* In what ways are the conversations in 1 and 2 above different? Can you give reasons for the differences?

Priest's Hole

In some old country houses you can still find little, secret hideaways, often near the chimney leading from the main fireplace. Here, in the days when it was often dangerous to be a Roman Catholic, priests were sometimes hurriedly hidden so that the soldiers would not find them.

Here is a poem about such a hideaway.

Sancta Maria,
Are they back yet again?
(Yes, horses and men and great dogs in the lane.)
Then off with the vestments,
Get the crucifix, plate . . .
(Oh, hurry now, Father
They beat on the gate.)
Do you stand in the chimney
And look down the flues,
I'm safe while you're watching the heretics' shoes;
And now for the ladder;
The hooks will hold fast,
Remember the trap-door, lad, right at the last . . .
The parcel of food, my missal, my beads . . .
You won't forget, lad, to straighten those reeds?
He hugged the child tight and then sprang for the rope,
Swayed forth and upward, lean hand stretched to grope
For the sill of the hole.
Then he trembling heaves
By wrists like white sticks, and he's under the eaves.
Now up with the panel, secure the trap-door
(Oh, quiet now, Father, they pace the hall floor)
And already the stamping of boots on the stairs,
While the priest's lips and fingers are fluttering their prayers.

Slow, slow weary hours drag their long way to night,
The soldiers depart;
The strained, tight,
Pale faces relax.

Quick – lift the trap-door . . .
He sleeps – see him nod . . .
He sleeps – surely?
Father! – Speak!
Mother of God!

Gregory Harrison

The most famous Priest's Hole was Little
John's hide at a house called 'Braddocks'. This
is how it was made:

1 Tiles were removed from the hearth of the
fireplace and a trap-door made.

2 The tiles were fixed to the trap-door.

3 A hole was dug out of the brick wall below.

4 A ledge was left for the person hiding to sit
on. The finished hole was only two feet wide
and five feet six inches high.

* If you wanted to hide someone in your house or school, and you
had a few days to prepare the hiding-place, where would you choose
to make the hide, and how would you do it?

Setting out a Letter

The greeting always begins with **Dear** and starts at the far left-hand side of the page. It is followed by the person's name and then a comma.

Put each new part of your address on a separate line and slightly further to the right.

Write the date in full. Start it under the address in line with the house number.

137 Warren Road,
Wilmington,
Devon.
22nd October 198—

Dear Andrew,

 I was very pleased to hear that ——

Best wishes,
Diane

The first word of your letter starts below the comma.

Your farewell begins with a capital letter and is followed by a comma.

Write your name clearly.

Decision

You have received the two letters below on the same day. One is from a very good friend, and the other is from the captain of a sports team which you want to play for.

Ward 3,
Chesterton Hospital,
Fordington.
22nd February 198–

Dear Chris,

You probably heard that I was taken to hospital after the accident I had last week. I've had an operation on my leg, but I'm O.K. I have to wear a plaster, but I'm all right. I reckon I'll be in here for a few weeks, though. The doctor said it would take time to set and he wants to do some tests or something.

The nurses are really nice, but I'm in a ward with mostly older people — they said the children's ward was overcrowded. I've got some games and books, though.

As Dad's away at the moment, he hasn't been to see me. Mum comes, of course, but she can't come every day because of her work.

I've got a great new game — Dad sent it — but I haven't played it much because the nurses are a bit busy and there's only a couple of patients who can get out of bed much and move around. I'm stuck in bed with my leg up in the air — you ought to see it!

If you're free on Saturday, it'd be great to see you. Mum can't come this weekend because of her work — they've got a big meeting on or something. Visiting is 2–3p.m. if you can make it.

See you,
Pat

FORDINGTON SPORTS & SOCIAL CLUB

PRIORY STREET
FORDINGTON
FD3 H67

22nd February 198—

Dear Chris,

I'm so glad you can play for us on Saturday. I expect you're very pleased to be picked for the team at last! It should be a close game, and it'll give you a chance to prove yourself. I know you've worked and trained hard for this opportunity for a long time.

The match starts at 2.30 p.m., so the minibus will pick you up in the Main Square at half past one. Don't be late!

See you on Saturday,
Stan

* You have to decide whether to visit the hospital or go to the match. Read the letters carefully again, then make your decision.

1. Write a letter either to Pat or to Stan explaining why you **cannot** come on Saturday. Whichever letter you write, you will have to make your reasons for not coming very clear: you do not want to offend your friend, nor do you want the captain of the team to think that you are unreliable. Try to put yourself in the position of the person receiving the letter, and think of the impression you want to make on him or her.

2. When you have written your letter, give it to someone else in the class to comment on, while you read and comment on his or her letter. The questions below may help you to make useful comments.

a. Does the writer make the reasons for his choice clear?

b. Does the letter make you sympathise with the writer?

c. Has the writer offered or promised to do anything to make up for not visiting the hospital or not coming to the match?

d. If you were the team captain, would you consider selecting this person to play in the future?

If you were the friend, would you feel hurt or offended because you were not visited?

WITCHES

Witches Galore!

A young boy (Kay) suspects that his governess, Sylvia Daisy, is really Mrs Pouncer, a witch. He decides to investigate her room.

He stood in the middle of the room, staring round him. It looked innocent enough, but was it? There were some strange little woodcuts on the bookshelves. When he looked at these more closely, they frightened him. Then there were some most strange playing-cards with Latin underneath their figures; he did not like the look of these. Then the books were not quite all that they might be. He only opened one; it had hieroglyphics instead of print. He put it back in its place and opened one of the portfolios of drawings. He did not like that at all: the drawings were of strange black figures upon red paper. He began to be very much afraid.

Then he thought that it was not very nice of him to come spying on her, when her back was turned; so he went out of the room.

Then he thought that Grandmamma Harker was right, that he ought to make sure that his home was not being used for witchcraft; so he went back again. He had not yet looked into the cupboard.

The cupboard (as he knew from Ellen) was really a room, being what was called a powdering chamber.

'And supposing,' he said to himself, 'supposing Mrs Pouncer is really her sister . . . and supposing she is in the powdering room, living there . . . that would account for the way the things go from the larder.' He looked through the cupboard keyhole; it was dark within; he could make out nothing. He flung the door wide open, crying 'Aroint thee, witch,' in case Mrs P. should be there.

Mrs P. was not there; no one was living there; the little room was in use as a clothes cupboard, but what were the clothes which hung from the pegs? Ah, what indeed?

There was a row of seven crooked pegs.

From each peg there hung a witch's complete outfit; thus:

1 long scarlet cloak.

1 black stick with a crooky handle.

1 tall, black, pointed shiny hat.

And attached to each hat there was something . . . he had to turn up the nearest hat to see what it was. It was marked inside Sylvia Daisy. The outside was a marvellous wax face of Mrs Pouncer.

'Now I know all about it,' he said. 'She is Mrs Pouncer; this is her mask . . . and look at all her magic and witch things on the shelf. She is a queen witch; she'll take a whole Archbishop to settle . . .'

He looked at the magic things on the shelf. There was a magic lantern which lit the cupboard like daylight when he touched a button; there were magic baskets labelled Wish; there were magic ladders and ropes, which pulled out, and out, and out, to any length you pleased; there were fox-eye and cat's-eye spectacles for seeing in the dark (he pocketed a pair of these); there was a gallon tin of Invisible Mixture; there were seven pairs of one league shoes; seven pairs of seven league shoes; and seven pairs of forty-nine league boots (these last were screwed down to keep them still). Then there were green and scarlet and yellow bottles, labelled Snake Bite, Dragon's Blood, and Pouncer's Best Bewitching Mixture. Then there was an ivory box labelled 'Ointment for turning little boys into tom-tits' (Kay did not touch this). Then there were bowls of gums and herbs for incantations. Then there were books, oh, such books with such titles:

Broomsticks, or the Midnight Practice.
Spells and How to Bind Them.
The Beginner's Merlin.
Merlin's 100 Best Bewitchals.
Were-Wolves, by one of Them.
Shape-Changing for All, by M. Le Fay.

And at the end of the shelf was a small red book: *Why I am a Witch* by Sylvia Daisy Pouncer.

'I say,' he thought, 'that is confession; she glories in it. I'll write to the Bishop. I don't care if it is sneaking. She has no business to be doing this kind of thing.'

'All the same,' he thought, as he looked at the row of scarlet cloaks, 'it would be rather sport to try on Mrs P.'s things.'

He hesitated for an instant, then he lifted the cloak from the peg; the outfit came down in one piece. He put it on before the mirror; the cloak was rather long; but when he said, 'I wish it were shorter,' it shrank to the right size. When he looked at himself in the glass, lo, he was Mrs Pouncer, hooky nose, crooky chin, and wicked, black, piercing eyes which could see further into things than his own eyes, as he very soon found; they were eyes like gimlets.

'I say,' he said, 'I look exactly like her. Now I will just watch myself conjure.' And at this he put his left hand on his heart and struck the crooky stick downwards on the floor.

Instantly he felt himself lifted into the air, off his feet, and through the open window. He had not time to catch hold of the rose trellis, he was carried so quickly past. He went floating along the drive, over the gate, over the Crowmarsh Estate, past Blinky's tree, over the manège where they were lunging the chestnut colt, then faster and faster, past the house where the poor mad lady lived, past the milestone on Racecourse Road, past the White rails of the course . . . on, on, on . . .

'O dear,' Kay cried, 'it's taking me straight to where all the witches are . . . and they'll turn me into a tom-tit. Stop, stop. I charge you to stop.'

It didn't stop, he didn't stop; he went faster and faster.

Soon the second milepost was passed; then the third, the stick began to point downwards towards a wooded hollow where the house called Russell's Dene stood. The stick was pointing towards the house; nothing that Kay could do seemed to have the slightest effect. 'I can't turn it or stop it,' he said. 'It's going straight to those windows.' The house was a big brick building of the time of Queen Anne. It had a gloomy, heavy look as though it were drunk and wore a wig.

'I'm going straight to where all the witches are,' Kay thought; 'they will bewitch me into a mouse and set the cat at me. O dear, O dear.'

The stick carried him swoop through one of the upper windows into a big, gloomy room, panelled to the ceiling. There were two open doors in this room, one on each side of Kay. People were talking just beyond one of these doors. Kay heard his governess' voice saying:

'What was that, that came through the window in the next room?'

from *The Midnight Folk* by John Masefield

* What do you think these words from the first paragraph mean?

> woodcut
> hieroglyphics
> portfolio?

* What do you think '**Aroint thee, witch**,' might mean, and why does Kay say it?

1. What do you think might happen next? Carry on the story.

2. Draw or describe some of the items which Kay found in the room and in the clothes cupboard.

3. What other things might have been inside the cupboard besides those which Kay sees? Make a list of some of these.

4. Invent some spells from *Spells and How to Bind Them.*

5. Write a page which might have come from one of the other books in the cupboard.

6. The twentieth century Mrs Pouncer might get about on a more modern version of the old-fashioned broomstick. Draw and label a design for an up-to-date broomstick. Your design might use modern inventions like rocket or jet propulsion, automatic pilot, radar scanners, and as many useful gadgets as you can invent.

7. Make drawings or models of things associated with witchcraft like: a witch; a bubbling cauldron; poison bottles; black cats; charm books; dragon's blood.

The Weird Sisters

(Three witches have met to make a magic potion)

1st : When shall we three meet again?
       In thunder, lightning, or in rain?
2nd : When the hurlyburly's done,
       When the battle's lost and won.
3rd : That will be ere the set of sun.
1st : Where the place?
2nd : Upon the heath.
3rd : There to meet with Macbeth.
1st : I come, Graymalkin!
2nd : Paddock calls.
3rd : Anon!
All   Fair is foul, and foul is fair;
       Hover through the fog and filthy air. . .
1st : Thrice the brinded cat hath mew'd.
2nd : Thrice and once the hedge-pig whin'd.
3rd : Harpier cries; 'tis time, 'tis time.
1st : Round about the cauldron go;
       In the poisoned entrails throw.
       Toad that under cold stone
       Days and nights has thirty-one
       Swelt'red venom sleeping got
       Boil thou first i' th' charmed pot.
All   Double, double, toil and trouble,
       Fire burn, and cauldron bubble.
2nd : Fillet of a fenny snake,
       In the cauldron boil and bake;
       Eye of newt and toe of frog,
       Wool of bat, and tongue of dog,
       Adder's fork, and blind-worm's sting,
       Lizard's leg, and howlet's wing –
       For a charm of pow'rful trouble,
       Like a hell-broth boil and bubble.
All   Double, double, toil and trouble,
       Fire burn, and cauldron bubble.
3rd : Scale of dragon, tooth of wolf,
       Witch's mummy, maw and gulf
       Of the ravin'd salt-sea shark,
       Root of hemlock digg'd i' th' dark,
       Liver of blaspheming Jew,
       Gall of goat, and slips of yew

Sliver'd in the moon's eclipse.
Nose of Turk, and Tartar's lips.
Finger of birth-strangled babe
Ditch-deliver'd by a drab –
Make the gruel thick and slab,
Add thereto a tiger's chaudron
For the ingredients of our cauldron.
All　Double, double, toil and trouble;
Fire burn, and cauldron bubble.
2nd :　Cool it with a baboon's blood,
Then the charm is firm and good.

from *Macbeth* by William Shakespeare

1. Look closely at the section beginning 'Thrice the brinded cat hath mewed . . .'
In this scene the witches are starting to mix their potion. They put into the cauldron all the nastiest and most evil things they can find. There are twenty-five items. Make a list; see if you can find them all.

2. *The Weird Sisters* is an extract from a play. The witches have to frighten the audience who must be made aware of their evil power. If you were directing this scene, what instructions and aids would you give to the actors playing the witches to help them to make their performance powerful and convincing?

3. Notice that there are **four** heavy beats in each line, and that the first line rhymes with the second, the third with the fourth, and so on:

'Eye of newt, and toe of frog,
Wool of bat, and tongue of dog . . .'

Write a similar scene, using your own list of ingredients.

4. Potions could be used to cure diseases or to wish them on people, or to put a curse on something or somebody. What would you use your potion for?

5. Try to invent some unusual potions: a potion for cursing a piece of machinery rather than a person, for example; or a potion to help people at school; or a potion to do good.

The Death of the Witch of Berkeley, 1065

'For my part, I have ever believed, and do now know that there are witches.'
Sir Thomas Browne 1605–1682

There resided at Berkeley a woman addicted to witchcraft, and of bad character. On a certain day, a jackdaw, which was a very great favourite, chattered a little more loudly than usual. On hearing which the woman's knife fell from her hand, her countenance grew pale, and deep groaning, 'This day,' said she, 'my plough has completed its last furrow; today I shall hear of, and suffer, some dreadful calamity.' While yet speaking, the messenger of her misfortunes arrived; and being asked why he approached with so depressed an air, 'I bring news,' said he, 'of the death of your son, and of the whole family, by a sudden accident.' At this intelligence, the woman, sorely afflicted, immediately took to her bed, and perceiving the disorder rapidly approaching the vitals, she summoned her surviving children, a monk and a nun, by hasty letters; and, when they arrived, with faltering voice, addressed them thus:

'Formerly, my children, I constantly administered to my wretched circumstances by demoniacal arts: although you cannot revoke the sentence already passed upon my soul, yet you may perhaps rescue my body, by these means: sew up my corpse in the skin of a stag; lay it on its back in a stone coffin; fasten down the lid with lead and iron; on this lay a stone, bound round with three iron chains of enormous weight; let there be psalms sung for fifty nights, and masses said for an equal number of days, to allay the ferocious attacks of my adversaries. If I lie thus secure for three nights, on the fourth day bury your mother in the ground; although I fear, lest the earth should refuse to receive and cherish me in her bosom.'

They did their utmost to comply with her injunctions, but alas! vain were pious tears, vows or entreaties; so great was the woman's guilt, so great the devil's violence. For the first two nights, whilst the choir of priests was singing psalms around the body, the devils, one by one, with the utmost ease, bursting open the door of the church, though closed with an immense bolt, broke asunder the two outer chains. The middle one, being more laboriously wrought, remained entire. On the third night about cock-crow, the whole monastery seemed to be overthrown from its foundations by the clamour of the approaching enemy. One devil, more terrible in appearance than the rest, and of loftier stature, broke the gates to shivers by the violence of his attack.

The priests grew motionless with fear, their hair stood on end, and they became speechless. He proceeded with haughty step towards the coffin, and calling on the woman by name, commanded her to rise. She replying that she could not on account of the chains: 'You shall be loosed,' said he, 'and to your cost!' And directly he broke the chain with as little exertion as though it had been made of flax. He also beat down the cover of the coffin with his foot, and taking her by the hand, before them all, he dragged her out of the church. At the doors appeared a black horse, proudly neighing, with iron hooks projecting over his whole back; on which the wretched creature was placed, and, immediately, with the whole party, vanished from the eyes of the beholders; her pitiable cries, however, for assistance, were heard for nearly the space of four miles.

from *Chronicle of the Kings of England* by William of Malmesbury

* What do these words mean: countenance, calamity, intelligence, demoniacal, revoke, adversaries, injunctions, entreaties, stature?

* What do you think is meant by 'sorely afflicted'?

* What does the witch mean when she says, 'Formerly, my children, I constantly administered to my wretched circumstances by demoniacal arts'?

* What does she mean when she says, 'My plough has completed its last furrow'?

* The witch is obviously very ill. What do you think is happening to her when she sees 'the disorder rapidly approaching the vitals'?

* What do you think the devil means when he says to the witch, 'You shall be loosed, *and to your cost'*?

* How does the witch know that she is going to die?

* The witch summons her surviving son and daughter to her. Why are they particularly suitable people to help her at this time?

* 'Her pitiable cries, however, for assistance, were heard for nearly the space of four miles.' The woman is obviously terrified and goes very unwillingly with the devil. What do you think of her? Should we feel sorry for her, or did she deserve her fate?

1. Imagine you are one of the monks or nuns present when the witch dies and is carried off. Write an account of what happened as you saw it yourself, and the effect it had upon you.

2. The writer of this account said that he had heard it from a man who was honest and respected and who swore that it was true. Imagine you met this man. What would you say to him, and what questions would you ask him, if you wanted to convince him that it could not be true?

3. Read again the quotation from Sir Thomas Browne at the beginning of this section. What might have happened to him to make him so certain that witches exist? Write a letter he might have written to a friend, explaining the reasons for his firm belief in the existence of witches.

The Witch's Curse

In this poem, a witch is calling up a powerful spirit (he in the poem) to help her make a curse.

Fire coom,
Fire gan,
Curling *smeak*   smoke
Keep oot o' t' pan.
There's a *tead* i' t' fire, a frog on t' hob,   toad
Here's t' heart frev a crimson *ask*;   newt
Here's a teath fra t'head
O' *yan* 'at's dead,   one
At never gat *thruf* his task.   through
Here's *prick'd* i' blood a maiden's prayer,   written
At t' *ee* o' man *maunt* see;   eye   may not
It's prick'd upon a yet warm mask,
An' *lapp'd* aboot a breet green ask,   wrapped
An' it's all for him an' thee.
It boils,
Thoo'll drink;
He'll speak,
Thoo'll think;
It boils,
Thoo'll see;
He'll speak,
Thoo'll dee.

* Look carefully at the last eight lines of the poem. What patterns do you find in the beginnings of the lines and in their endings? How do these patterns help to build up to the frightening climax of the last line?

* The poem is written in Yorkshire dialect. What does **dialect** mean?

1. Try to write a poem or curse in which you build up to a similar climax at the very end.

2. Rewrite the poem in ordinary modern English.

3. Write a conversation in which two or three characters, speaking in the dialect of the part of the country you come from, discuss a strange experience.

Words

Here is a list of words connected with witchcraft:

prophetess, seer, sooth-sayer, sorceress, clairvoyant, hag, witch, wizard, spectre, spook, magician, charmer, exorcist, conjuror, mumbo-jumbo, spell, charm, curse, potion, hoodoo, voodoo, hocus-pocus, demon, diviner, harridan, monster, obsession, possession, talisman, scarab, wishbone, wand, file, amulet, philtre, bell-book-and-candle, oracle, enchantment, incantation, astrologer, warlock, superstition, sorcery, Sybil, satyr, ghoul, witchery, ghastly, uncanny, odd, diabolical.

* Find out the meanings of some of the words you don't know, by using a dictionary.

1. Can you put the words into groups according to their meanings? For example:

words which are the names for people concerned with magic and sorcery;
words which might help to describe such people and what they do;
words for the things which they might use in their art.

2. Try making a shape-poem of some of the words. Here are two examples to help you. Add words not included in the list, if you wish.

odd
hag
witch
spook
potions
wizards
harridans
obsession
hocus-pocus
mumbo-jumbo
– a-witch's-hat –

c
\
a
\
r
v
o
y
a
n
t
seer
wizard
voodoo
hoodoo
oracle
amulet
talisman
diabolical
astrologer
possession
enchantments
superstition

Superstitions

* Many people are superstitious.

Some superstitions are said to bring good luck;
some are said to bring bad luck;
others guard against misfortune.

Which categories do the following belong to?

to touch wood
to break a mirror
to throw a horseshoe over your shoulder
to say 'Rabbits' on the first day of the month
to throw salt over your left shoulder
to walk under a ladder
to say 'Bless you!' when someone sneezes
to open an umbrella indoors
to wear (if you are a girl going to your wedding):
  'Something old, something new,
  Something borrowed, something blue.'

1. Think of as many superstitions as you can and put them into the same three categories. Which group is the largest?

2. Using the list you have made, write a story about someone whose belief in superstitions is so strong that his or her life is completely dominated by them.

Suppose You met a Witch

Suppose you met a witch . . . There's one I know,
all willow-gnarled and whiskered head to toe.
We drownded her at Foot Ten Bridge
last June, I think, –
but I've often seen her since at twilight time
under the willows by the river brink,
skimming the wool-white meadow mist
astride her broom o'beech.
And once, as she flew past, with a sudden twist
and flick of the stick she whisked me in
head over heels, splash in the scummy water
up to my chin –
ugh! . . .
Yet there are witless folk will say
they don't exist.
But I was saying – suppose YOU met a witch,
up in that murky waste of wood
where you play your hide and seek. Suppose
she pounced from out a bush,
she touched you, she clutched you,
what would you do? No use
in struggling, in vain to pinch and pull.
She's pinned you down, pitched you into her sack,
drawn tight the noose.

There's one way
of escape, one word you need to know –
W – A – N – D. Well,
What does that spell? . . .
They learnt it years ago,
two children – Roland and Miranda – clapped
in a witch's sack and trapped
just as you might be. HE
was a mild and dreamy boy, musical
as a lark – in the dark
of the jolting sack he sang. SHE
was quick in all she did, a nimble wit, her brain
busy as a hive of bees at honey time.

And Grimblegrum – that was the witch's name –
jogged them home.

This was the usual sort, a candy villa
with walls of gingerbread, porch and pillar
of barley sugar. She kicked the gate
and the licorice-beaded door,
undid the sack string and tipped them
on the glassy glacier-minted floor.
As Roland fell, his boot struck
the crystal paving stones and chipped them.
Like an angry rocket
she launched at him. Miranda
sprang for the magic wand
and pinched it from her pocket.
  'Tip, tap – O house of cake,
  be a cloud-reflecting lake
  with me and Roland, each a swan
  gracefully afloat thereon!
  And, deeper than e'er plummet sounded
  Grimblegrum the witch be drownded!'
'Twas done – look there, d'you see two swans
a-gliding, serene and cool
upon that heaven-painted pool
over the blue sky, over the floating clouds that shine
like snow-white fleeces?
Sudden, in burst of bubbles the witch popped up
and shivered the cloud to pieces.
'I'll gobble you yet!' she gulped,
but all she gobbled was water as with windmill arms
she thrashed and lashed at them. No swimmer,
she would have sunk like a boulder below,
had not a felon crow,
black-hearted as his feather, swooping, dipping,
hoisted her by the belt and borne her, boggy,
drooping, dripping,
home.
  'She'll follow us – no time to loose –
quick we must fly!' Miranda cried.
Heavily they rose;
far over field and forest, with whining wing
all night through
till dawn of day they flew.

Meanwhile the Grimble-witch, now dry,
had put on her seven league boots and (do or die)
seven miles at a step came galloping,
gulping, 'Gobble you yet, I'll gobble you yet!'
The swans heard her cackle and a thudding where she stepped –
down by a screen of trees they swept,
down to a lonely roadside out of view.
    'I'll change myself to a rose of crimson hue,
set in a prickly hedge,' Miranda said,
'and, Roland, as for you,
you'll be a piper, and the magic wand
your flute.'

    Not a second too soon – for the witch's boot
touched ground beside them. And she croaked:
    'O glorious goriest rose!
    I have sought you from afar,
    how I wonder what you are!
    You may mock me from on high,
    but I'm the spider, you're the fly!
    Ha! ha! ha! ha! ha! ha!'

    And she gaped at that glorious and goriest of roses
with the greediest of eyes and the nosiest of noses.
Again she spoke:
'Good piper, this rose how dainty it would look
if I stuck it in my cloak!
May I pluck it?'
    'Good lady, you may. And I'll play
to you the while.' And Roland smiled,
for his was a MAGIC flute,
each golden note entrancing –
none could listen without dancing.

                                One note one,
                            she spun like a top.

                            Two notes two,
                        she hopped and couldn't stop.

                        Three notes three –
                    and into that thorny thistle-y tree
                    with a hop, skip and a jump went she.

Tootle-toot! sang the flute
and up went her boot
and down again soon
to the tantivy tune.
Every thorn and twig
did dance to the jig
and the witch willy-nilly-
each prickle and pin
as it skewered her in
was driving her silly.

Hi!
  ho!
    shrieked she,
and tickle-me-thistle! and prickle-me-dee!
and battered she was as she trotted and tripped,
and her clothes were all torn and tattered and ripped
till at last
all mingled and mangled,
  her right leg entangled,
    her left leg right-angled,
firm as a prisoner pinned to the mast,
she
  stuck
    fast.

Silence, not a sound as Roland wiped
the sweat from his brow. Then gently with his pipe
he touched the rose. Out leapt Miranda
to the ground. Hand in hand,
chuckling, through the wild wood
away home they ran.

That same evening, a cowman passing by
paused by a roadside bush to cut a switch.
He heard a cry;
turning, saw in a hedge nearby a prickly witch
who screamed and yelled and hissed at him and spat.

So he put a match to the hedge. And that was that.

Ian Serraillier

Suppose **you** met a witch?

Alphabetical Order

The word **alphabet** comes from Greek and is made from the names of the Greek letters **alpha** (our letter a) and **beta** (our letter b).

Encyclopaedias, dictionaries, telephone directories and most indexes are arranged in alphabetical order.
   If words in an alphabetical list begin with the same letter, like **orange** and **opera**, the word whose second letter comes first in the alphabet is placed before the other word in the list.
So,
   opera comes before
   orange.
   If words in an alphabetical list begin with the same three letters, like **order** and **ordinary**, the word whose fourth letter comes first in the alphabet is placed before the other word in the list.
So,
   order comes before
   ordinary.
   You can see how this works in the list below where the letter in each word which has been used to fix the order is printed in bold type:
   opera
   operation
   opinion
   opponent
   oppose
   optimist
   option
   or
   orange
   orchestra
   order
   ordinary

1. Working with someone else in the class, decide where the following extra words should be placed in the list above:

   ordeal, oral, opposite, orchard, open.

Lists of people's names are often put into alphabetical order according to their surnames; this is done on school registers and in telephone directories. If two or more people have the same surname, Anne Croft and Jane Croft, for example, because A comes before J in the alphabet, **Croft, Anne** comes before **Croft, Jane.**

2. Write the names below in alphabetical order:

Albert Kelly   Elizabeth Orr
Helen Riley   Nada Hussein
Kishore Singh   Judith Norton
Ruth Nolan   Angela Harrison
Conrad Peters   Alexander MacPherson
Andrew North   Joanne Peters
Frank Mason   Kevin Lauder

Names like McPherson and McDougall, are usually pronounced the same as MacPherson and MacDougall, and, in a written list of names, they always appear as if they were spelled **Mac**, as in the list below:

McDonald, Angela   Mace, Rebecca
MacDonald, Jennifer   MacFarlane, Arthur
McDougall, Janet   McFarlane, Peter

3. Write out the list above, adding the following names in correct alphabetical order:

McFadden, Terrence   Machen, Catherine
McEwan, Carla   Macey, Denise
MacHale, Eric   Machinder, Pauline
McHaigh, Stanley

Names or titles which begin with the word **Saint**, like Saint John's Hospital and Saint Margaret's School, are often written as St John's Hospital and St Margaret's School. In an alphabetical list, however, they always appear as if they were written **Saint**, as in the list below:

Sainsbury, Raymond   St Paul, Nichola
St Andrew's Church   Sainty, Geoffrey
St John Ambulance   Salisbury, Jessica
St Mary's College

4. Write out the list above, adding the following names in correct alphabetical order:

St George's Hotel   Saies, Mohammed
Saint Anthony's Club   Salen, Frank
Sails, Harry   Sainty, Peter

In a library, fiction — novels, stories and so on — is arranged in alphabetical order according to the authors' surnames. If there is more than one book by the same author, the book whose title will appear first in an alphabetical list is usually placed first.

5. Suppose you are in charge of a section of the fiction books in a library. You have been given the books listed below to arrange correctly on one of the shelves. Rewrite the list in alphabetical order as they should appear on the shelf.

Author	Title
Christopher Leach	The Water-Tower
Joan Lingard	The Twelfth Day of July
Bill Leigh	Sink-Hole
Benjamin Lee	The Man in Fifteen
Elinor Lyon	The Floodmakers
Marjorie Lloyd	Fell Trek
Penelope Lively	Astercote
Astrid Lindgren	Mardie
Penelope Lively	The Whispering Knights
Noel Langley	The Land of Green Ginger
Hilda Lewis	The Ship that Flew
Cecil Day Lewis	The Otterbury Incident
Ann Lawrence	The Conjuror's Box
Samantha Lee	The Quest for the Sword of Infinity
Alec Lea	To Sunset and Beyond
Jack London	The Call of the Wild
Joyce Langlin	The Seekers
C. S. Lewis	The Last Battle
David Line	Mike and Me
Joan Lingard	Across the Barricades
Josephine Lee	The Fabulous Manticora
Madeleine L'Engle	A Wrinkle in Time
Eric Linklater	The Wind on the Moon
Robert Leeson	The Demon Bike Rider
Jane Langton	The Diamond in the Window

LOST?

Holiday children missing

Two children, Allan and Joanne Bedford, aged eleven and twelve, were reported missing yesterday. They have been staying in Wennington with their aunt, Mrs Mary Bishop, raised the alarm last ... Joanne failed to return ... today. ... for ... ren. ... ning ... y, tall ...

Cliff mystery baffles council

Wennington Borough Council officials revealed today that they have received several reports of noises coming from the cliffs at Arnsby Head. Local residents are worried that the cliffs may be unsafe.

Mr James Shaw, for the council, said that the cliffs had been surveyed in October last year, following similar reports last summer, and found to be safe.

"We found no indications of subsidence or disturbance in the cliff face," commented Mr Shaw today. He did reveal, however, that the network of caves at the foot of the cliffs could ... eyed at that time, owing to a ... ptionally high ... y out a ...

Mr and Mrs Bedford,
, Rose Terrace,
Dartby,

WENNING

August

8 Sunday   Went to the beach and the zoo. ... miles of golden sand, but the ... isn't too crowded with people - just on ... calling Allan "Gregor" - its the name of one of the af ... alike - always rushing about and annoying people ...

9 Monday
Rained. Went ... the town for a while and then played games in ...

10 Tuesday   Spent the afternoon at ... Allan's idea! It was a ... He said it was a personal hot-dog ... The man on the rifle range was ... really rich-looking person, so in the ... really wanted it, he was just fed up ... Anyway, the man on the ... and ... him ... have ...

We went on the big wheel ... and Allan kept laughing ... was sick after, so we're even ... know it was the wheel ... and Allan got six hits ... busy talking to this ... an just reached over ... I touched ...

11 Wednes ...
model ... ago. Th ... the ligh ... but I ...

Beach o ...

Lost on Holiday

Allan and Joanne Bedford have gone to stay with their aunt and uncle in Wennington, a seaside town, for a week's holiday.

Some of the things that happen to them during their holiday are revealed in the documents that follow.

POST CARD

CORRESPONDENCE

Having a great time! We've explored most of the town and we're going to the beach again on Thursday. Beach is a bit small, but there are lots of little rock-pools and the cliffs have got caves in them. See you on Sunday.
Love
Allan and Joanne
xxx

Mr and Mrs Bedford,
23, Rose Terrace,
Dartly,
Warwickshire.

Post card from Allan and Joanne to their parents

11, Gladstone Ave.,
Wennington-on-Sea,
11th August

Dear Jenny,

Allan and Joanne seem to be enjoying themselves. I'm pleased and a bit relieved, really. I thought they might be bored, but they're very keen on exploring the place. We took them to the beach and the zoo on Sunday and they loved it. Harry enjoyed himself too!

They've both been very sensible, so I think it's all right to let them go exploring on their own. You said they'd be all right looking after themselves and I'm sure they will be. Allan's got a very inquiring mind, hasn't he? He's been asking Harry lots of questions about local history — especially shipwrecks and smugglers! I think he must have got interested in some of the things at the museum — it's quite a good one, really.

We're looking forward to seeing you for dinner on Sunday. If the weather's nice, we could have a drive down the coast in the afternoon, before you go back with the kids. What do you think?

Love,
Mary

Letter from the children's aunt, Mary Bishop, to their mother, Jenny Bedford

Extract from Joanne's diary

August

8 Sunday Went to the beach and the zoo. The beach is O.K. Its not exactly miles of golden sand, but the rock pools are good and it isn't too crowded with people – just enough. I've started calling Allan 'Gregor' – it's the name of one of the apes. They're really alike – always rushing about and annoying people! Ugly too.

9 Monday

Rained. Went out into the town for a while and then played games indoors.

10 Tuesday Spent the afternoon at the fair. We went on the big wheel – Allan's idea! It was a bit scary and Allan kept laughing when I screamed. Anyway, he was sick after, so we're even. He said it was a poisoned hot-dog, but I know it was the wheel. The man on the rifle range was really weird. Allan got six hits, so he asked for a prize, but the man was so busy talking to this really rich-looking person, so in the end Allan just reached over and took a little teddy-bear thing off the counter. I don't think he really wanted it, he was just fed up with this man ignoring him. Anyway, the man on the stall went mad. He grabbed the bear and said it wasn't a prize, and then he wouldn't give Allan anything at all. He was really rude. As we went away, I saw him give the bear to the man he was talking to, so it <u>must</u> have been a prize really. But I didn't tell Allan.

11 Wednesday

Went to the museum today. They've got a fantastic model of the town as it used to be hundreds of years ago. The guide said there used to be lots of wrecks before the lighthouse was built. Allan says there were smugglers too, but I don't think he <u>knows</u> that.

Beach again tomorrow. We're going to explore the caves.

CASH SALE INVOICE

No 02150

Date..12..19.8.

£   p

Torch — 90

Receipt from a shop, found
on the floor of Allan's room
by Mrs Bishop

Extract from *The Wennington Gazette*, Friday 13 August

Holiday children missing

Two children, Allan and Joanne Bedford aged eleven and twelve, were reported missing yesterday. They have been staying in Wennington with their aunt, Mrs Mary Bishop. Mrs Bishop raised the alarm last night after Allan and Joanne failed to return home for their tea. Mrs Bishop said today, 'I am very worried. They went to the beach for the day. They're both very sensible children, I'm sure they wouldn't run off or anything like that.'

Allan is described as a fair-haired boy, tall for his age. When he left the house he was wearing blue jeans and a yellow pullover and was carrying a small rucksack. Joanne has short dark hair and was wearing grey corduroy jeans and a blue jumper.

High tide today: 9.32 p.m.
High tide tomorrow: 10.07 a.m.

Cliff mystery baffles council

Wennington Borough Council officials revealed today that they have received several reports of noises coming from the cliffs at Arnsby Head. Local residents are worried that the cliffs may be unsafe.

Mr James Shaw, for the council, said that the cliffs had been surveyed in October last year, following similar reports last summer, and found to be safe.

'We found no indications of subsidence or disturbance in the cliff face,' commented Mr Shaw today. He did reveal, however, that the network of caves at the foot of the cliffs could not be fully surveyed at that time, owing to a spell of bad weather and exceptionally high tides.

'The only thing we can do is carry out a further survey,' said Mr Shaw, 'but I doubt whether anything new will be found.'

Extract from news broadcast on local radio, 9.00 a.m. Saturday 14 August

'Police at Wennington-on-Sea said today that they would like to interview a middle-aged couple who were seen in a motor launch in the bay at Wennington yesterday near a large yacht moored close to the entrance to the bay. Following information received by the police last night from a group of ornithologists who had been studying sea-birds near Arnsby Head, it is believed that the owners of the yacht may have information about the two children reported missing on Thursday night.'

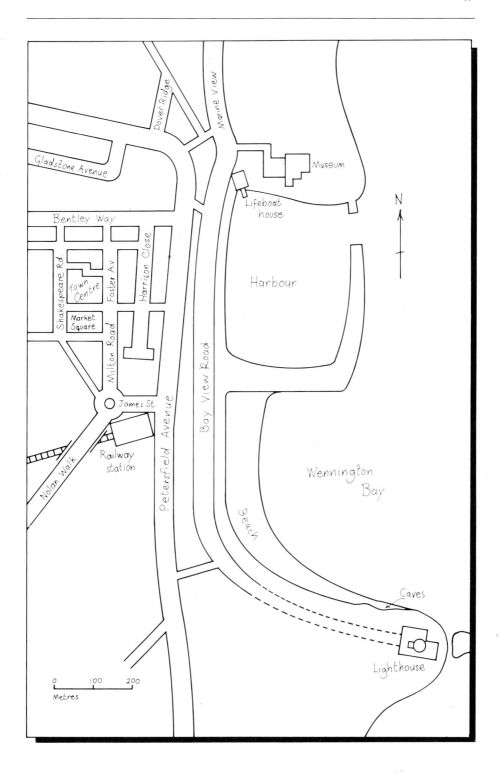

Ten quick questions

* Who were Allan and Joanne staying with?
* What is the name of the town where they are staying?
* Who is Jenny Bedford?
* Who is Harry?
* Which two places did they visit on the Sunday?
* What did Allan take from the counter of the rifle-range of the fair?
* On which day did Allan and Joanne go to the beach on their own?
* Mrs Bishop found a receipt in Allan's room. What was it for?
* On which day was Allan and Joanne's disappearance reported in the newspaper?
* How do we know that the children are still missing on Saturday morning?

1. Write the full story of what happens, as if you were Allan or Joanne. Your story should start with their trip to the beach on Thursday. Your account must fit the known facts given in the documents, but you may, of course, use ideas of your own as well. Whatever happens to Allan and Joanne in your story must be believable — the reader will lose interest if the story is very far-fetched. Remember also that Allan and Joanne are people like you; if they get lost, or trapped, or threatened, they will be very frightened and worried, even if they try not to show this.
It may help you to organise your story if you divide it into days or chapters.

2. Construct a mystery of your own. Your material should include the following:
> a postcard,
> a letter,
> an extract from someone's diary,
> a newspaper report.
You may add as many other items, or more reports, letters and so on, as you wish.

Make sure that all the material you provide is convincing. Look back at the material here to help you set out letters and write news reports correctly.

Police Report

Police Constable Wood has collected evidence concerning the arrest of a man who is alleged to have robbed a Post Office in the town of Bildale.

∗ Look at the map of part of Bildale and the extract from PC Wood's notebook below.

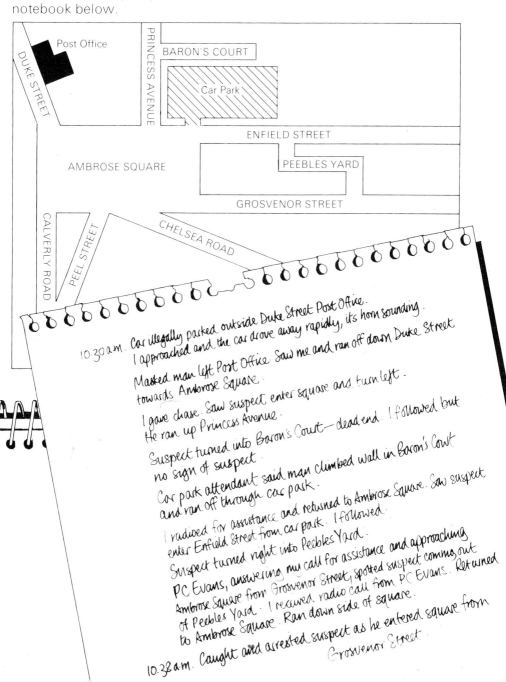

10.30 a.m. Car illegally parked outside Duke Street Post Office.
I approached and the car drove away rapidly, its horn sounding.
Masked man left Post Office. Saw me and ran off down Duke Street
towards Ambrose Square.
I gave chase. Saw suspect enter square and turn left.
He ran up Princess Avenue.
Suspect turned into Baron's Court—dead end. I followed but
no sign of suspect.
Car park attendant said man climbed wall in Baron's Court
and ran off through car park.
I radioed for assistance and returned to Ambrose Square. Saw suspect
enter Enfield Street from car park. I followed.
Suspect turned right into Peebles Yard.
PC Evans, answering my call for assistance and approaching
Ambrose Square from Grosvenor Street, spotted suspect coming out
of Peebles Yard. I received radio call from PC Evans. Returned
to Ambrose Square. Ran down side of square.
10.32 a.m. Caught and arrested suspect as he entered square from
Grosvenor Street.

Assume that you are Police Constable Wood. It is your job to turn the information from the notebook and the map into a report for your senior officer, Inspector Hammersleigh, to read out in court.

Inspector Hammersleigh was not satisfied with your last report for him. Here is *that* report with the Inspector's comments.

BILDALE CONSTABULARY

Station

Division

19

Subject

Submitted by

Sergeant
Inspector

I followed the suspect into the street. Then I went up to him and then I asked the suspect for his name and address, but the suspect ran off and so I gave chase and arrested him at the corner of Peel Street, and the man was arrested and then he was taken to the Police Station in a police van.

I can't read this in court! Each stage of the incident must be clear so that the magistrate can follow it easily. Do not repeat words too often: there are too many and s and then s here. Rewrite.

E.K. Hammersleigh.

FORM   1

A friend helped you to rewrite that report. Below is your revised report which the inspector accepted.

BILDALE CONSTABULARY

.... Station

.... Division

.... 19 _____

Submitted by

....
Sergeant
Inspector

Subject

I followed the suspect into the street. I went up to him and asked him to give his name and address. The suspect ran off and I gave chase. I caught and arrested the man at the corner of Peel Street, where he was escorted to a police van and driven to the Police Station.

EKH

FORM 1

1. Write your report on the Post Office raid. You may find it useful to work on a rough copy first. Take Inspector Hammersleigh's advice: make your report clear and do not repeat yourself.

Capital Letters

A capital letter is used:

at the beginning of a sentence;
for the name of a person or place;
for the title of a book, play, film or television programme;
for trade names, and names of companies and organisations.

Some of the words below begin with capital letters. Can you explain why?

newspaper

Cardiff   shop   cash register

valve   The Daily Mirror   Elastoplast   dance

petunia   Miss Malarkey   magazine   Concord   shrimps

feet   The Koran   British Rail   three-ply wool

Gatwick Airport   onion   lobster

Jameson Street   ITV

The Railway Children

Which of these words should begin with a capital letter?

baby-sitter

robert smith   book

avondale road   london   dictionary

mr jones   ship   rhubarb   transistor   disco

the beano   kellogg's corn flakes   tonsils   the bible

birmingham   the titanic

wednesday

i

Sentences: full stops and capital letters.   ●

A sentence begins with a capital letter and ends with a full stop. Here are some examples:

The old man patted his dog lovingly.
All my friends had gone.
Yesterday, my uncle came home from Pakistan.
Each railway wagon rattled as it crossed the points.

In each of the examples above, an **action** is completed.

In each of the examples below, a **complete statement** is made about a person or a thing:

> John is asleep.
> The old horse was lame.
> Your aunt will arrive soon.
> A giraffe cannot talk.

There are also groups of words which begin with a capital letter and end with a full stop, but which do not include a complete action or make a complete statement. However, these can also be called sentences because their **meaning** is complete. Here are some examples:

> Hello.
> Sale now on.
> Ticket holders this way, please.
> Two for the price of one.

Which of the following are sentences, and which are not?

1. The dog bit the man who was patting him.
2. As we were walking across the street.
3. You'll be sorry you said that.
4. Graham's motor-bike fell apart.
5. As he opened the door, he felt a sharp pain in his leg.
6. Stamped and addressed envelope enclosed.
7. Swaying in the wind, rustling as they moved.
8. While we were asleep in the tent.
9. Because she was afraid, she opened the door very softly.
10. He was very angry.
11. No walking on the grass.
12. We must decide what to do.
13. They were all around us.
14. There isn't time to get there now.
15. Running down the lane, jumping the hedges, galloping across the fields.
16. Room for three more upstairs.
17. If the animals are hungry or upset.
18. This attitude isn't good enough.
19. Because he was alone.
20. Goodbye.

The full stops and capital letters have been missed out of this piece of writing. Put them in.

> on tuesday i was sitting in my garden reading the daily mail when a pancake came flying over the hedge it landed with a loud plop on my cat bonzo she was most annoyed she attacked the pancake as if it had been a mouse i asked my neighbour, mr patement, what was going on he apologised and said that his little girl had just learned how to make pancakes at school that morning he had been demonstrating to her how to toss them in a frying pan the cat stalked into the house looking very pained and dignified.

Sentences: question marks and exclamation marks.

Questions, commands and exclamations are also sentences.

When you write a question, the full stop is replaced by a question mark. For example:

> What is the weather like?
> Does your dog always sleep there?
> Are you enjoying your work?
> How are you?
> Which flavour would you like?
> Who was that?

When you write an exclamation, the full stop is replaced by an exclamation mark. For example:

> For heaven's sake!
> Mind what you're doing!
> Look out!
> A lot of help you are!
> Oh, no!
> What a shame!

Some of the sentences below need a question mark; some need an exclamation mark; some need a full stop. Which needs which?

1. Good heavens, she's fallen off the cliff
2. My grandad has come to live with us
3. Are you always as late as this
4. I'm losing my balance; look out
5. Football is a favourite game with many boys
6. It was six-thirty before I got in from school last night
7. Why do some people seem to need more sleep than others
8. Who was the first person to climb Mount Everest
9. Clear off
10. Is this the queue for the ferry, please
11. Many people think of the Lake District as one of the most beautiful places in England
12. A great friend you turned out to be

Sentences: commas

A **comma** is used to show a small pause in what is being written. For example, in a list:

James was wearing three tee-shirts, a pair of trainers, green socks, a pair of old jeans and a denim jacket.

Sara's collection of treasures included an old necklace from her granny, a scratched Beatles' record, two gerbils, a Valentine from an American friend and a key ring with a plastic whistle on it.

The commas in the sentences above separate the items in the lists. Notice that the last item in the list is separated from the one before it by the word **and**, not by a comma.

Complete the following lists by adding suitable items, putting in the commas in the correct places:

1. The best teams in Football League Division One are
2. Of all the records in the Top Twenty, I like
3. The most boring programmes on TV are
4. The meals I most like to eat include
5. When I was in the infants' school, my favourite teachers were

In some sentences, commas are used like brackets. Here is an example:

> When we were in the New Forest, where we went for our summer holiday, we visited the National Motor Museum.

In that sentence, the section **where we went for our summer holiday** could be left out and the sentence would still make sense:

> When we were in the New Forest we visited the National Motor Museum.

If we extend a sentence in this way by pushing words into the middle of it, the words have to be 'eased in' by the use of commas. Here are some more examples:

> My brother, who is an exceptionally tall man, can't really sit comfortably in my car.

> As we were coming through the entrance hall, tired out after all our work, my mother fainted.

Below, on the left, are some sentences. On the right are some sections which could be 'eased' into them. They are not lined up with the sentence they would fit in with best. Sort them out and make new sentences, not forgetting to put in the two 'easing' commas.

1. Sergeant Morrison stumbled into the yard.	who considered her maiden-name to be very unpleasant
2. When I went to see the headmaster I was sick all over the carpet.	including Mrs Foster
3. The winner held the cup high above his head.	limping badly because of his injured leg
4. Gladys Hackenschmitt married Humbert Schnickendorf.	melting in the sun
5. My uncle Ted surprisingly bought me a record for Christmas.	a really steep one
6. The others in the group were miles ahead of us.	who had just moved into his new office
7. The ice-cream oozed over the back seat of our car.	who is usually a very mean person.
8. That last hill always seemed to take hours to climb.	Jamie Salkey

Sentences: tags

When people are talking they often add words or groups of words to their main statement or question. For example:

Yes, please, I'd love some jam.
It's great, *isn't it?*
Look here, John, you can't go on like this, *can you?*
Well, *sir*, it was there yesterday.

The words in italics are often called tags. Tags do not add to the simple meaning of the sentence, but they can, for example, emphasise what is being said; show the politeness of the speaker; make it clear who is being talked to.

All tags are separated from the main parts of the sentence, and from one another, by commas. Here are some examples:

Oh, Jane, what are you doing?
Hello, uncle, how are you?
You like it here, don't you?
No, I'm not going, thanks.
You shouldn't do that, you know.

Copy out the examples below, and add the necessary commas:

1. Well that's what I think anyway.
2. I made a mess of that didn't I?
3. Hey you stop that!
4. Yes I'd like some more please.
5. Well what are you going to do Emma?
6. But Mum you said I could go didn't she Dad?
7. Yes I've got to go haven't I?
8. Oh no that's torn it!
9. You will be careful won't you dear?
10. Anyway you can't have any so there!

Speech Marks

When you write down what someone says, his words are placed between speech marks (sometimes called inverted commas):

'I am very tired.'

Nowadays, in printed books, it is usual to use single speech marks but it is also quite correct to use double speech marks: "I am very tired." Note that the full stop at the end of what the speaker says goes **inside** the speech marks.

If this sentence is extended because you want to show who is speaking, note what happens:

> 'I am very tired,' said Uncle Bernard.

The full stop after **tired** has become a comma. The sentence now ends after **Bernard** so that is where the full stop must go.

If what someone says is a question or an exclamation, for example:

> 'Why are you late?'
> 'Go away!'

and you wish to extend the sentence, a full stop is placed at the end of it, but no other changes are made to the punctuation:

> 'Why are you late?' she asked.
> 'Go away!' the man shouted.

Write out the following, putting in the necessary punctuation.

1. It's only a few miles to the next village she explained
2. The trouble with most people is that they don't listen said Paul
3. Can you help me carry these please he asked
4. Oh it's you again is it she asked
5. Get lost he shouted
6. Oh do stop whining said the woman to her child
7. At the third stroke the time will be three forty seven precisely said the speaking clock
8. Where are you going she called
9. Stand at ease bawled the sergeant-major
10. The next programme follows in two minutes said the announcer
11. On your marks get set go called the starter
12. I'm sorry there are no seats left she apologised

When you write a conversation between two or more people, always begin each person's speech on a new line and **indent** it: that is, start the line one or two centimetres in from the margin. This is so that the reader can see at a glance where one person's speech finishes and another person's speech begins.

Read the conversation below and then continue it:

> Keith came in muttering under his breath.
>> 'What's the matter with you?' asked his mother.
>> 'I've just got thrown off the bus,' Keith said angrily.
>> 'Well, it probably serves you right,' said his mother. 'I expect you were fighting.'
>> 'But I wasn't fighting! Somebody pushed me!'

Apostrophes – one **he's I'm you're**

Apostrophes are used to show that a letter (or letters) has been missed out of a word. Here are some examples:

do not	*may be written*	don't
have not	*may be written*	haven't
has not	*may be written*	hasn't
does not	*may be written*	doesn't
you are	*may be written*	you're
they are	*may be written*	they're
I have	*may be written*	I've
they have	*may be written*	they've
he is	*may be written*	he's
I am	*may be written*	I'm
would have	*may be written*	would've
should have	*may be written*	should've
it is	*may be written*	it's

Add the necessary apostrophes to the following:

1. 'Its a long way to the house, isnt it?' Grandad complained as he struggled into my car. 'Ive always said they built the houses too far from the station. If it wasnt for the lift you give me, I dont think Id manage to get all that way home. Mind you, it wasnt like this when I was a youngster. Hasnt it all changed now? Havent you noticed how its all changed? No, I suppose youre too young arent you?'
   He closed the door of the car, and we drove off.

2. The men would have gone after the horses, but they couldnt find the lanterns and so they werent able to see.
   'Its no good,' said George, 'well never find them in the dark.'

'Theyll be right across the other side of the moor by the time its light,' said Jane.

'It cant be ten yet,' said Graham. 'Theyll be wandering about all night.'

'You shouldve mended that stable door when I told you to,' said George. 'None of this wouldve happened.'

Apostrophes – two **Helen's Simon's**

If you want to show that something is owned by, or is part of, someone or something, you can write it like this:

> The car belonging to the woman was almost new.
> The muddle was caused by the mistake of the computer.

However, there is another, quicker way of writing this; you can add an apostrophe and an **s** to the name of the owner. So, the examples above could be written:

> The woman's car was almost new.
> The muddle was caused by the computer's mistake.

Here are some more examples:

The roof of the temple shone in the sun.	*could be written*	The temple's roof shone in the sun.
The best trick of Houdini was an under-water escape.	*could be written*	Houdini's best trick was an underwater escape.
General Turner complained that the equipment belonging to his army was out of date.	*could be written*	General Turner complained that his army's equipment was out of date.
Admiral, the dog owned by the night watchman, was not injured in the fire.	*could be written*	Admiral, the night watchman's dog, was not injured in the fire.
The mother of Judy Fonseca was pleased with the work of her daughter.	*could be written*	Judy Fonseca's mother was pleased with her daughter's work.
The acting of the children is excellent.	*could be written*	The children's acting is excellent.

In the last example above **children** is the plural of **child** — that is, it refers to more than one child.

However, most plurals end in **s**, for example: girls, horses, brothers, cars and so on. Instead of adding 's to these plurals to show that something is owned by or is part of them, you add an apostrophe only. For example:

The den belonging to the girls was empty.	*could be written*	The girls' den was empty.
We repainted all the stables of the horses.	*could be written*	We repainted all the horses' stables.
The bedrooms belonging to my brothers are both larger than mine.	*could be written*	My brothers' bedrooms are both larger than mine.
We could tell that the exhaust pipes of several cars were leaking.	*could be written*	We could tell that several of the cars' exhaust pipes were leaking.
The water rose higher, lapping round the waists of the rescuers.	*could be written*	The water rose higher, lapping round the rescuers' waists.
In the supermarket the hands of the shelf-fillers were aching from working so fast.	*could be written*	In the supermarket the shelf-fillers' hands were aching from working so fast.

Re-write each of the following sentences to include 's or ':

1. The father of this puppy was a well known prize-winner.
2. The lids of the boxes were all nailed down.
3. The cages of the lions and the tigers need cleaning out.
4. We were late because the radiator of the car boiled dry.
5. This area is reserved for cars belonging to firemen.
6. Some driftwood lay at the edge of the sea.

Add the missing apostrophes to these sentences:

1. I've got at least an hours homework to do tonight.
2. Where are the ladies cloakrooms, please?
3. That mans swimming costume looks like a babys nappy.
4. What have you done with todays paper?
5. In the middle of the show both clowns trousers fell down.
6. The seagulls skimmed above the peoples heads.

FLOODS

If London Flooded . . . ?

You have been asked to speak for the Greater London Council on a television programme, answering questions about the threat of floods in London. Below are several pieces of information about the possible flooding, and the interviewer has given you lists of questions which might be asked on the programme. Using the information given, prepare your answers. You should **either** write the answers out in full **or** write them in note form and then act out the interview with a partner or in a small group.

Opposite is the first piece of information, based on a poster which the Greater London Council has produced.

Here is the first list of questions.

1. How will people in the flood risk areas know that a flood is expected?
2. What should people who live in the flood risk area do when they hear the warnings?
3. Are there any preparations which people who live in these areas should make in advance?
4. What should people who work in the flood risk area do if they are warned that a flood is expected within the next four hours?
5. What should someone do who does not live in the flood risk area, but is stranded there when the sirens sound?

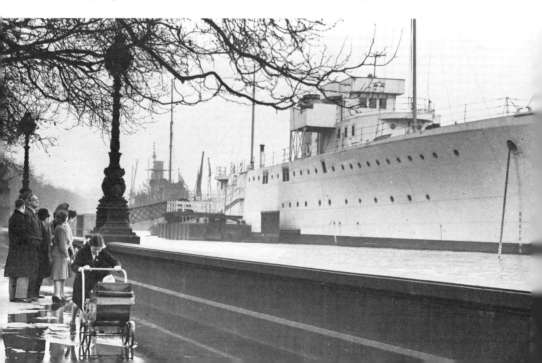

IF LONDON FLOODED TOMORROW WHAT WOULD YOU DO?

This is what you **must** do if you live, work or travel in the Flood Risk Area.

FIRST PUBLIC WARNING

About 4 hours before flooding official warnings will be issued on Radio, T.V & Public Notices.
Buses and trains will start to be withdrawn after 2 hours.

Go home immediately.

LAST PUBLIC WARNING - Sirens

About 1 hour before flooding sirens will sound.

Go upstairs and stay put.
Do **not** travel in the flood risk area.
Stay tuned to local radio.

This map shows the risk area

Thames Flood Prevention
Low-lying areas bordering the River Thames

Areas below Trinity High Water (+11.40 OD (Newlyn)).
about 24 square miles

FLOOD RISK AREA

Stations where certain services will stop short after the sirens.
<u>All</u> public transport will stop running in the Flood Risk Area after the sirens.

IF IN DOUBT CONTACT YOUR LOCAL TOWN HALL OR EMPLOYER NOW FOR MORE DETAILS.

The Threat of Floods in London

Central London was last flooded in 1928 when 14 people drowned. In 1953 came the disastrous flooding of the East Coast and Thames Estuary with a toll of 300 lives and if this flooding had reached central London's highly populated low-lying areas the result could have been horrifying beyond measure.

There are two continuing reasons for the danger of flooding and one special threat which occurs from time to time. The continuing reasons are that London is slowly sinking and that the tides in general are rising, and the special threat is from surge tides.

Not only is central London sinking on its bed of clay but over the centuries Britain itself is tilting. Scotland and the north-west are rising and south-eastern England gradually dipping downward at a rate of about one foot every hundred years. The increase of high tide levels has been going on for at least a century and records indicate that over the last hundred years tide levels have risen by over two feet at London Bridge.

Surge tides which are the special threat occur under certain meteorological conditions. When a trough of low pressure moves eastwards across the Atlantic towards the British Isles, the sea beneath it rises above the normal level thus creating a hump which moves eastwards with the depression. If the depression passes the North of Scotland and veers southwards into the North Sea, extremely dangerous conditions may be created. A surge happens when this mass of water coming from the deep ocean reaches the relatively shallow southern part of the North Sea. The height of a surge may be much increased by strong northerly winds.

Dangerous conditions may also occur when a depression – after crossing Britain – moves quickly into the southern part of the North Sea, but this kind of surge is smaller than one that comes from the North of Scotland.

If a high surge reaches the bottleneck between South East England and the Low Countries, and enters the Thames Estuary on top of a high tide, then there can be real flood danger along most of the tidal Thames.

Such a flood in London could paralyse the central part of the underground railway system, knock out power, gas and water supplies, cut vital telephone and teleprinter services and severely hit thousands of homes, shops and factories, businesses and buildings. It could take months to get London functioning normally again.

Here is the second list of questions.

6. When was London last flooded?
7. Why is there a continuing risk of flooding in London now?
8. Approximately how much higher are tides in London now than they were when the city was last flooded?

9. What is a surge tide? (You may refer to the map on page 69 in answering this question if you wish — a copy of it can be provided in the television studio.)
10. When might a surge cause serious flooding?
11. What would be the main effects of a serious flood in London?
12. What sorts of problems would people stranded by the flooding have to face?
13. Would there be any special problems for the elderly, the very young or the handicapped?
14. How long would it take for everything to get back to normal after the floods?

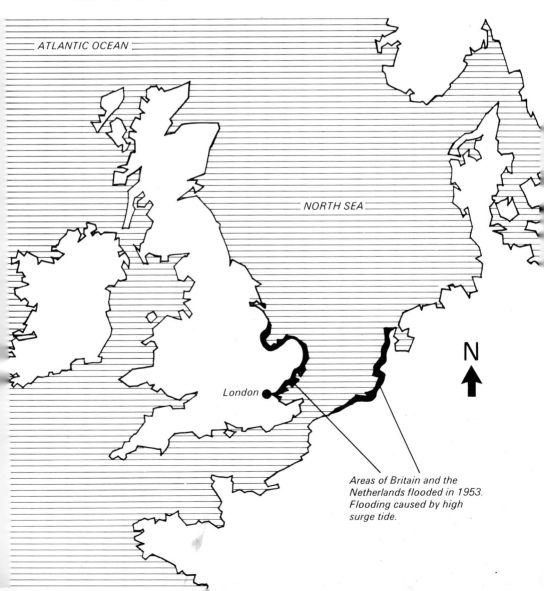

Areas of Britain and the Netherlands flooded in 1953. Flooding caused by high surge tide.

The Thames Barrier

In order to prevent a flood, the Greater London Council are taking two precautions: they are erecting a movable barrier at Woolwich and in company with the Thames, Anglian and Southern Water Authorities, raising walls and embankments along the Thames, downriver to the Outer Estuary.

The barrier is a series of separate movable gates built side-by-side across the river. Each gate is pivoted and supported between concrete piers which house the operating machinery and control equipment.

Closing the barrier when required will seal off the upper Thames estuary from the sea. When not in use, the barrier gates rest out of sight in their curved recesses in concrete sills in the river-bed, allowing free passage of river traffic through the openings between the piers.

If a dangerously high tidal surge threatens and an order to close is given, the engineer in charge will start operations which will result in the gates being swung up through about 90 degrees from their river-bed position into a vertical defensive position, forming a continuous steel wall facing downriver ready to stem the tide. Barrier closure itself would take only about 30 minutes.

The width of the barrier from bank to bank will be about 520 metres, with four main openings each having a clear span of 61 metres. The four main gates will be massive. Each is designed as a hollow steel-plated structure over 20 metres high and weighing with counterweights about 3,300 tonnes. Each will be capable of withstanding an overall load of more than 9,000 tonnes.

adapted from *Thames Flood Defences*
issued by the Greater London Council

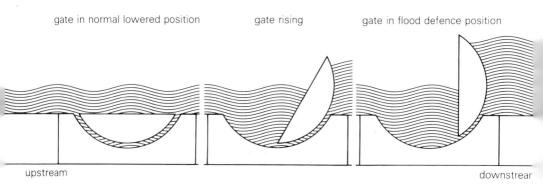

gate in normal lowered position   gate rising   gate in flood defence position

upstream   downstrear

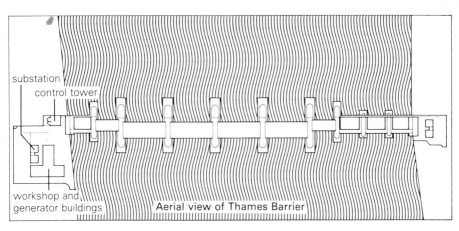

substation
control tower
workshop and generator buildings
Aerial view of Thames Barrier

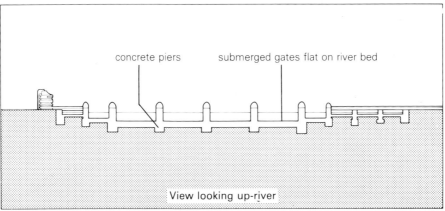

concrete piers   submerged gates flat on river bed

View looking up-river

Here is the third list of questions.

15. What is the Greater London Council doing to try to prevent this flood?

16. How wide is the barrier from bank to bank?

17. What are the gates of the barrier made of?

18. How much does each gate weigh?

19. How many main openings are there in the barrier?

20. How wide is each opening?

21. Normally, when there is no danger of flooding, how will ships and barges be able to get past the barrier?

22. In an emergency, how long would it take to close the gates of the barrier?

23. Won't the barrier just make the flooding worse *below* Woolwich?

24. What happens if there is a power-cut in the Woolwich area just before a flood? Would the barrier be put out of action?

Storm Surge

Peter, a teenage boy, and a friend, Susan, have been helping one of Peter's brothers, Martin, to look after their father's pub for the evening. The pub is close to the sea on the East coast and it is a stormy night. Martin has just left.

Peter and Susan listened to the sound of the old car fading in the distance as it reached the bridge, then there was only the wind screaming and the pounding of huge waves, the smack of water as it came over the wall and hit the ground, the slap of the spray as it drenched roofs and windows . . .

Peter's thoughts were interrupted by a strange noise coming from the floorboards. At first he thought it was a mouse scratching, then it became more continuous, a hiss like escaping gas. He went to the stove, but all the taps were turned off. He looked again at the floor, and watched in horror as water came bubbling through the cracks between the boards, at first in long lines, but they were rapidly spreading into a lake that would soon cover the floor.

'Susan! Look!'

She shrieked with fright, then ran to the window and threw back the curtains. The clouds had lifted and there was a full moon. There was no land any longer. The sea, black and silver in the moonlight, stretched from the kitchen window to the horizon. It was swirling past at speed, rising every minute, not in great waves and torrents, but in an almost orderly fashion, like a bath filling. The walls had held, here at least, but they were not high enough.

'Peter! We can't get out! I shan't get home! What'll we do?'

Do? What on earth should they do first? They must not panic. He banged his hands against his head; no thoughts would come.

'Take the money out of the till and get it upstairs. I'll try and get hold of Dad.'

He went into the hall and dialled David's number, but before his brother answered, Susan was back. The water was up to their ankles, black and freezing cold.

'What now?'

The important thoughts came to him. 'There's candles in the larder. And matches. And take the brandy from the bar. And any rugs or cushions you can find. Get them all upstairs. David?'

'Candles?'

'The water will fuse the electricity. David? The sea's in the house; it's almost up to my knees. Where? In the pub, you fool. Where's Dad?'

'They've gone.'

The phone went dead. The water must be in the wires somewhere. What now? What now? Martin. He dialled Martin's number, hoping against hope that it was David's phone that had failed, not his. There were three separate flats in Martin's house, with one phone they all shared on the landing. Answer it, Martin! He must be home by now. Susan raced downstairs and floundered past him. 'I've left my bag and coat in the kitchen,' she said.

'Martin, the water's in the pub. I'm up to my knees . . . police? No, I didn't think. You'll ring them? I'm getting upstairs –'

There was a tremendous crash as the three doors of the pub burst open simultaneously, a deafening wrenching noise of splintering wood, and a great wall of water surged towards him. The lights all flickered, and went out.

'Martin!' He was shouting, terrified. 'Save me! Save me! We're drowning!'

*   *   *

Peter struggled towards the kitchen. The water was up to his neck, the cold of it stupefying. When he tried to swim he was pushed back by the force of the torrent against the wood of the staircase. He clung to the bannisters. His head felt as if it didn't belong to him and the muscles of his chest seemed rigid as if they were trying to stop his lungs taking in air. Several things banged into him. It was so dark that he was not sure what they were, but he thought they came from the kitchen, the plastic bread-bin, a milk jug. From the bar came the jingling brittle sound of dozens of bottles all crashing into each other. Then the flood began to lose its strength; the flow slackened and it was rising more slowly. He swam towards what he thought was the kitchen door, and banged his head on the wood of its frame. There was still some space between the water and the ceiling, but he was afraid it would not be there for long. He lashed out with one arm trying to find the lintel and hit a cup and saucer floating on the surface, and the saucepan he had used earlier to make the cocoa. Then his right foot struck the door-knob, and he was able to heave himself up onto the top of the door, his foot still on the handle, his head touching the ceiling.

'Susan! Where are you?' he shouted.

'Here!' Her voice was quite near him. 'I thought you'd . . . I climbed on the table, then pulled a chair onto it. Now I'm standing on the chair.'

'But . . . why are you so near me?'

'The sea's pushed the table against the wall and jammed it against something. It's not floating; perhaps it's my weight.'

'We must get out. There won't be much air left soon.'

'How can we?'

'Swim of course. Can you follow me?'

'I can't swim.'

from *Storm Surge* by David Rees

* What is the first sign of the rising flood?

* Look through the first half of the extract. How do you know that the water is rising very quickly inside the pub?

* Working with someone else, discuss the following:
    How many sensible things can you find that Peter and Susan did?
    How many things they did were not so sensible, do you think?

* What signs are there in what Peter thinks, says and does that show that he is panicking?

* It is not only the depth of water which makes it difficult for Peter to get to the kitchen. What other obstacles or problems does he encounter?

* What do you think Susan was going to say when she said, 'I **thought you'd** . . .'? Why didn't she finish saying it?

* In an emergency such as this one, who do you think is more useful: a person who gives orders, or one who carries them out? Why?

1. Peter tells Susan to move the following items upstairs: **money, candles, matches, brandy, rugs and cushions**. Put these items in what you think would be their order of importance to Peter and Susan. Explain why you think Peter suggested each one.

2. If you were either David or Martin, receiving Peter's telephone call, what would you do when the phone was cut off? Write the story of what happens from Martin's or David's point of view starting from the interrupted telephone call.

3. Write the story of someone caught in a flood, including his or her thoughts and feelings as well as describing the scene.

Escape from the Floods on Canvey Island 1953

Survivor :   I woke up and heard a funny noise and wondered what it was. I got out of bed and when I looked outside I was in a sea. Well, I jumped out quickly and got a few clothes on and came in the sitting-room and of course the water was coming up and up and up, and I jumped on the bed settee first, and the water got up to my chest, and I thought I have got to get up on something higher than this. Well, this table was floating round the room and I got hold of the thing and pulled it along to the fireplace and, er, threw myself across it and of course the water was washing over me then, so I got on my feet and stood up and, er, there I stood until late Sunday.

Interviewer :   You stood on the table?

Survivor :   I stood on the table top, pressed against the mantelpiece, until late Sunday; I should imagine it must have been about four or five o'clock. I was so exhausted by standing, I tried to get down on the table to sit but I lost me balance and me feet and legs went in the water and the water then was coming right up. I sat like that until I was rescued on Tuesday.

Interviewer :   On Tuesday?

Survivor :   On Tuesday about four o'clock.

Interviewer :   But you must have been there for three days.

Survivor :   Yes. I was there for three days.

Interviewer :   But did you have anything to eat?

Survivor :   No, I couldn't get anything. I was in the water and couldn't get at anything.

Interviewer :   Nothing to drink?

Survivor :   No, nothing at all. It was drink I wanted. But, er, the milk was on the table . . . if I thought . . . if I only could get that but I couldn't; and I had a nice little bottle of whisky my daughter brought me home from Ireland.

Interviewer :   Where was that?

Survivor :   That was in the dressing-table drawer in the bedroom.

Interviewer :   That is the place to keep it.

Survivor :   Yes well, I couldn't get it so I had nothing at all until they rescued me and took me to hospital.

Interviewer :   You were conscious the whole time, you remember?

Survivor :   Well, no, I kept losing myself but I knew I'd got to keep me senses, otherwise I should have gone into the water. I fought against sleep and I fought against unconsciousness.

from a BBC radio interview

* How can you tell that this is spoken, not written, language?

* How would you describe the tone of what the survivor says? For example, is it boasting, modest, exaggerated, matter-of-fact, hysterical, or what?

* In what ways do you think the survivor behaved sensibly?

* What were the main dangers the survivor had to face?

* What were the main discomforts the survivor suffered?

* If you were the interviewer, what other questions would you have wanted to ask?

Imagine that an area near you or a place which you know well is flooded.
1. Working with someone else if you wish, write some articles for the local newspaper for the day after the flooding. If you like, you could use some of the headlines given below:

HAVOC AS FLOODS HIT TOWN CENTRE
LIZ ROWS THEM TO SAFETY
THE LAST BUS THAT BECAME A LAST REFUGE
FAMILY CLINGS TO ROOF
STRANDED – THEY STILL REFUSED TO BE RESCUED
ARMY CALLED IN TO SAVE FARMERS AND ANIMALS

2. Write the script of a radio documentary about the flood, including interviews with rescuers, people affected by the floods, police and firemen and so on, as well as news stories, on-the-spot reports and details of what is being done to help people.

Future Flood

In this extract from a science fiction story, a radio script-writer explains what happens in London as the tides rise to levels of more than fifteen metres, as a result of the melting of the polar ice-caps.

The first day passed safely. On the evening of the highest water a large part of London settled down to wait for midnight and the crisis to pass, in a sullenly bad-tempered mood. The buses were all off the streets, and the Underground had ceased to run at eight in the evening. But plenty of people stayed out, and walked down to the river to see what there was to be seen from the bridge. They had their show.

The smooth, oily surface of the river crawled slowly up the piers of the bridges and against the retaining walls. The muddy water flowed upstream with scarcely a sound, and the crowds, too, were almost silent, looking down on it apprehensively. There was no fear of it topping the walls; the estimated rise was twenty-three feet, four inches, which would leave a safety margin of four feet to the top of the new parapet. It was pressure that was the source of anxiety.

From the north end of Waterloo Bridge where we were stationed this time, one was able to look along the top of the wall, with the water running high on one side of it, and, to the other, the roadway of the Embankment, with the street lamps still burning there, but not a vehicle or a human figure to be seen upon it. Away to the west the hands on the Parliament clock-tower crawled round the illuminated dial. The water rose as the big hand moved with insufferable sloth up to eleven o'clock. Over the quiet crowds the note of Big Ben striking the hour came clearly downwind.

The sound caused people to murmur to one another; then they fell silent again. The hand began to crawl down, ten past, a quarter, twenty, twenty-five, then, just before the half-hour, there was a rumble somewhere upstream; a composite, crowd-voice sound came to us on the wind. The people about us craned their necks, and murmured again. A moment later we saw the water coming. It poured along the Embankment towards us in a wide, muddy flood, sweeping rubbish and bushes with it, rushing past beneath us. A groan went up from the crowd. Suddenly there was a loud crack and a rumble of falling masonry behind us as a section of the wall, close by where the *Discovery* had formerly been moored, collapsed. The water poured through the gap, wrenching away concrete blocks so that the wall crumbled before our eyes and the water poured in a great muddy cascade on to the roadway. . .

(A year after this first flooding, the writer goes to look at another familiar London landmark.)

One day we walked down to Trafalgar Square. The tide was in, and the water reached nearly to the top of the wall on the northern side, below the National Gallery. We leant on the balustrade, looking at the water washing around Landseer's lions, wondering what Nelson would think of the view his statue was getting now.

Close to our feet, the edge of the flood was fringed with scum and a fascinatingly varied collection of flotsam. Further away, fountains, lamp-posts, traffic-lights, and statues thrust up here and there. On the far side, and down as much as we could see of Whitehall, the surface was as smooth as a canal. A few trees still stood, and in them sparrows chattered. Starlings had not yet deserted St Martin's church, but the pigeons were all gone, and on many of their customary perches seagulls stood, instead. We surveyed the scene and listened to the slip-slop of the water in silence for some minutes.

from *The Kraken Wakes* by John Wyndham

* What precautions against the flood have been taken before the evening's events described here?

* 'It was pressure that was the source of anxiety.' What happens to demonstrate that the crowd's anxiety was justified?

* Find words or phrases which demonstrate the mood of the watching people, before and during the flood.

* In the third and fourth paragraphs of this extract, the writer mentions the clock several times. Why does he do this, and why does he describe the movement of the hand of the clock in such detail just before the flood surges in?

* What is flotsam?

* Why is it more effective for John Wyndham to describe the flooding of a very well-known place like Trafalgar Square, than the centre of a much smaller, less well-known town?

* In the last paragraph what details help to show how strange and shocking the scene appears to the writer?

1. Suppose that other well-known places (or places well known to you) have been flooded very badly. Describe the scene before, during and after the floods.

Sounds

Read the poem below, which is a modern version of part of a very old poem—*Sir Gawain and the Green Knight*.

> Then from the court the clamour came
> Of hammering hooves and heavy tread,
> The ring of iron and rattle of chain.
> Within, the men were hushed and still,
> As stern and sure into the hall there strode
> A massive man, tree-tall and broad,
> His long, lithe limbs well made and strong.
> He was a warrior wild: from head to heel
> He shone with steel. And all his look
> Was gaunt and grim. And all his flesh,
> His long, loose locks, and all his armour too:
> All shone the same – bright green in hue.

The writer has used the **sounds** of words as well as their meanings in describing this strange man. Two or more words in each line begin with the same sound: for example, Of hammering hooves and heavy tread.
This is called **alliteration**.

Sometimes the meaning of a word is contained in or re-inforced by its sound: for example, words like **clamour, hammering,** and **rattle** in the poem.
This is called **onomatopoeia**.
There are many examples of onomatopoeia, words like **bang, slap, whisper, murmur,** and **sigh.**

* Say these words below aloud and then see if you can put those words which sound alike into groups. Some words may go into more than one group.

rustle	crackle	whimper	whisper	crunch
smooth	whine	mumble	pluck	prattle
crash	creak	chatter	smack	plop
rumble	sigh	grumble	snarl	crack
mutter	pop	soothe	rattle	purr
slither	murmur	snigger	sneer	bubble

* Compare your groupings with those of others in the class. Discuss your reasons for putting words into one group rather than another.

Writers, especially poets, often use words like these to help create atmosphere. Here are two extracts from a poem by Alfred Tennyson. In the first extract, a knight — Sir Bedivere — who is wearing armour, is climbing amongst rocks:

> Dry clashed his harness in the icy caves
> And barren chasms, and all to left and right
> The bare black cliffs clanged round him as he based
> His feet on juts of slippery crag that rang
> Sharp-smitten with the dint of armed heels . . .

In the second extract, Sir Bedivere leaves the rocks and sees before him a lake, shining under the moon:

> And on a sudden, lo! the level lake,
> And the long glories of the winter moon.

* Which words in these two extracts help to show the noise or atmosphere of the two scenes by their sound?

1. Write a description of one of the following, as a poem if you wish:

> a fire engine rushing through the streets of a city,
> a lonely, deserted stretch of moorland in winter,
> a storm at sea,
> a long goods train travelling through a cutting,
> a snake moving through a swamp,
> a monster moving through a thick forest.

GAMES

Favourite Game

This is an excerpt from a story set in and around the city of Durham, at the beginning of this century. Dick Ullathorne and Peter Fairless are the sons of miners at Branton Colliery.

Just over the rise there was a long lane with sycamore and stunted oaks that led to their favourite playground. It was a long sloping field of furze that ended in a rectangular clayey pond with one open side. Their favourite game was to work their way cautiously up to the top of the field, dodging from clump to clump as if they were surrounded on all sides by enemies, and then, having reached the upper end of the field, to go steeplechasing down, furiously and recklessly, leaping over every bush that was in their way. It was a law of the game not to shirk a jump, and when they came to the bottom their legs were always scratched and prickled. They would throw themselves down on the banks of the pond until their wind came back. It was a glorious game. In spite of the occasional appearance of a gamekeeper or a farmhand this little field was their kingdom, a territory that no other boys seemed to want, a land so much their own that they began to give names to its features. The little pond was christened Lake Ullathorne, the steeplechase course was the Fairless Ride, and the lane leading to them the Venturers' Way.

They could not wade in the lake. It was too muddy, and the water was too cold; but they sailed logs across it, pulled up the dead shoots of mare's-tail, threw berries at floating leaves, and drove little flotillas of sticks from side to side. Then, when they were tired of these games, they turned to the little pools that had formed all round the pond in the clayey soil after the rain, little lakes of clear rain-water through which you could look at the brown and yellow leaves laid layer on layer on the floor of the pool. The curled and coloured leaves seemed preserved there, as if they had been laid up in isinglass. They plunged their hands into the cold water, touched the berries and acorns lying there, built banks around the pools, gave them all names, but, always under some compulsion which they did not understand, kept the beautiful underwater patterns undisturbed.

One day when they were kneeling over one of their little water-museums they both had the feeling that they were being watched; and when they looked up they saw, looking steadily and fearlessly at them, a stoat, its inquisitive head high, its fine white breast clearly visible. For a moment Dick had the strange feeling that it had recognised him. They looked into each other's eyes. Then the stoat turned slowly away and was gone as silently as it had appeared. Day after day they waited for it to come again, but it never reappeared. Dick could not get rid of the feeling that it had known this was their kingdom, and had left it to them.

from *The Bonny Pit Laddie* by Frederick Grice

∗ 'It was a glorious game.' What makes this sort of game so much fun?

∗ Why do you think that Frederick Grice writes that the boys went 'steeplechasing down' rather than just 'running down'?

∗ The boys don't seem to mind that 'their legs were always scratched and prickled' in the game. Why didn't they mind?

∗ Which of the following words best expresses how the boys felt during the game: excited, exhilarated, thrilled, elated, intoxicated, delighted?

∗ Why does the writer describe the tiny pools as 'little water-museums'?

∗ Why should the boys feel that they ought not to disturb the beautiful underwater patterns in the pools around the pond?

∗ How can you tell that the boys think of this field as theirs?

1. Imagine the owner of the field has told the children to stop playing there. Write or improvise the conversation that takes place between Dick and Peter after the owner has gone. Include in the conversation their reasons for feeling that they ought to be allowed to play there.

Children's Games

* Look closely at the pictures and those on the next two pages. [You might find it helpful to work in pairs.]

* How many different games can you count being played?

* How many of the games can you name?

* Try to invent names for the games that are new to you.

* Here is a list of names of games which children used to play at the end of the nineteenth century:

> stip-bit; over-backs; tally-ho; three lives; tip-cat; bulldog; cocky-five-jacks; knocky-nine-door; dobbers; knuckletoe; dribble-hole; barley biscuits; hi-acki; egg-if-you-budge; duckstone; tag; kick-the-block; stag-a-rag; rileo; save-all; pig's snout, walk out.

Could any of these nineteenth century names be used for the games shown in these pictures?

* Choose one of the games in the pictures. Decide how you think it might have been played. Ask yourself, for example, how many people can play. Are the players to be put into teams? Do they need to use a ball or some other object? Do they have to mark out a pitch? Does the game need boundaries, like walls or hedges?

When you have done this, write out the rules, so that anyone can understand how to play the game. Make sure that you get your rules in the right order, putting the most important ones first.

Here, to help, are the rules of a well-known game:

a. Between four and twenty players can play.

b. The game is played on a flat, hard area, such as a school yard or a street.

c. One person is made 'it' and has a ball.

d. The other players run away while the one who is 'it' counts to ten.

e. The player who is 'it' may not run while carrying the ball, but may run while bouncing it.

f. The player who is 'it' throws the ball at the others and tries to hit one of them above the knee. If he hits someone, that player then helps him to get the rest onto his side in the same way.

g. Players who are being chased may not handle the ball, except with clenched fists.

h. The last player to be hit by the ball is the winner.

(The name of this game varies from place to place. What is it called where **you** live?)

Dicky, Dicky, Shine the Light

This story is set in a town during the Second World War.

The blackout was no longer a matter to be observed scrupulously in our district. But if chinks of light were tolerated flashing beams could still excite policemen and air-raid precaution wardens and lots of other adults with leanings toward public responsibility. So there was added a deeply satisfying, extra danger to the nightly episodes of Dicky, Dicky, Shine the Light.

The game was close to the proportions of a tournament. It was no slight, single-night affair; it could take a week to work through it, the tension building all the time. The framework was utterly simple: one boy with an electric torch, the rest scattered and calling him to catch and identify them in the glare of the light. But among these terraces, with alleys, yards, dustbin alcoves, outhouses, dog kennels, raintubs, hedges, broken walls and dumped gas-stoves, all menacing with shadow in the sourly misted night, the hunt was elaborate with stealth and deception. The torch had to be used sparingly, to conserve the battery and to delay interference from adults. We had great skill in hiding, using the shapes of shadow, calling the names and running full-speed into some blind blackness, inviting a chase. Timidity meant failure. Chance could be calamitous: a door suddenly opened to let out a wedge of light; an irritated dog; a loose tin accidentally kicked.

Hiding is always accompanied by fear, even in games; the two instantly associate. In the dark even the most familiar setting can intimidate. Like all our games Dicky, Dicky was essentially an ordeal.

from *The Great Apple Raid* by Arthur Hopcraft

* Why might adults, particularly those 'with leanings toward public responsibility' want to stop the children's game?

* What does the writer mean when he says 'Timidity meant failure'?

* 'Hiding is always accompanied by fear, even in games.' The children are frightened during the game, but they enjoy it, and play it often. Do you play any games which are a little frightening as well as fun?

* Can you think of any other activities in which people seem to enjoy being a little frightened?

* Why do you think that fear can sometimes increase enjoyment?

* 'Like all our games Dicky, Dicky was essentially an ordeal.' In what ways might the game described in *Favourite Game* also be called an ordeal?

1. Write a story which begins with a game played outside in the dark. You might base the story on your own experiences of playing in the evening in the streets or fields.

2. Write about hiding from other people, or about being the hunter.

3. Here are some titles for other stories you may write:
     Trapped!
     The Quarry
     It's Only a Game
     The Chase.

Hide and Seek

Call out. Call loud: 'I'm ready! Come and find me!'
The sacks in the toolshed smell like the seaside.
They'll never find you in this salty dark,
But be careful that your feet aren't sticking out.
Wiser not to risk another shout.
The floor is cold. They'll probably be searching
The bushes near the swing. Whatever happens
You mustn't sneeze when they come prowling in.
And here they are, whispering at the door;
You've never heard them sound so hushed before.
Don't breathe. Don't move. Stay dumb. Hide in your blindness.
They're moving closer, someone stumbles, mutters;
Their words and laughter scuffle, and they're gone.
But don't come out just yet; they'll try the lane
And then the greenhouse and back here again.
They must be thinking that you're very clever,
Getting more puzzled as they search all over.
It seems a long time since they went away.
Your legs are stiff, the cold bites through your coat;
The dark damp smell of sand moves in your throat.
It's time to let them know that you're the winner.
Push off the sacks. Uncurl and stretch. That's better!
Out of the shed and call to them: 'I've won!
Here I am! Come and own up I've caught you!'
The darkening garden watches. Nothing stirs.
The bushes hold their breath; the sun is gone.
Yes, here you are. But where are they who sought you?

Vernon Scannell

* What phrases and sentences in the poem suggest that the person hiding is uncomfortable?

* The poet says a good deal about the things that the child hears, feels and smells. Look at the poem again and explain why these senses are important here.

* One single line near the middle of the poem contains four sentences. Find the line and say why you think the poet has written it like this.

◉ 'The darkening garden watches. Nothing stirs.
The bushes hold their breath; the sun is gone.'
How can a garden 'watch' and bushes 'hold their breath'?
What do you think the child is feeling at this moment?

∗ The boy or girl in the poem calls out 'I've won!' What spoils this
sense of achievement?

1. Try to imagine what the person who was hiding feels, now that the
others seem to have abandoned the game. Write or improvise the
scene in which this child meets the others later.

seek
seek	hide	hide	hide	hide	hide	hide	hide
hide	seek	hide	hide	hide	hide	hide	hide
hide	seek	hide	hide	hide	hide	hide	hide
hide	hide	seek	hide	hide	hide	hide	hide
hide	hide	hide	seek	hide	hide	hide	hide
hide	hide	hide	seek	hide	hide	hide	hide
hide	hide	hide	hide	seek	hide	hide	hide
hide	hide	hide	hide	hide	seek	hide	hide
hide	hide	hide	hide	seek	hide	hide	hide
hide	hide	hide	hide	seek	hide	hide	hide
hide	hide	hide	hide	seek	hide	hide	hide
hide	hide	hide	hide	hide	seek	hide	hide
hide	hide	hide	hide	hide	hide	seek	hide
hide	hide	hide	hide	hide	hide	hide	seek
hide	hide	hide	hide	hide	hide	seek	hide
hide	hide	hide	hide	hide	seek	hide	hide
hide	hide	hide	hide	hide	hide	seek	hide
hide	hide	hide	hide	hide	hide	hide	seek
hide	hide	hide	hide	hide	hide	hide	**find**

Curiouser and Curiouser!

A girl, Alice, has found her way into a very strange land. In this extract from the story of her adventures, Alice meets the Queen, who, with a large party of relations, guests and soldiers, is about to play a game of croquet.

'Can you play croquet?' shouted the Queen.

The soldiers were silent and looked at Alice, as the question was evidently meant for her.

'Yes!' shouted Alice.

'Come on, then!' roared the Queen, and Alice joined the procession, wondering very much what would happen next.

'Get to your places!' shouted the Queen in a voice of thunder, and people began running about in all directions, tumbling up against each other; however, they got settled down in a minute or two, and the game began. Alice thought she had never seen such a curious croquet-ground in all her life; it was all ridges and furrows; the balls were live hedgehogs, the mallets live flamingoes, and the soldiers had to double themselves up and to stand upon their hands and feet, to make the arches.

The chief difficulty Alice found at first was in managing her flamingo: she succeeded in getting its body tucked away, comfortably enough, under her arm, with its legs hanging down, but generally, just as she had got its neck nicely straightened out, and was going to give the hedgehog a blow with its head, it *would* twist itself round and look up in her face, with such a puzzled expression that she could not help bursting out laughing: and when she got its head down, and was going to begin again, it was very provoking to find that the hedgehog had unrolled itself, and was in the act of crawling away: besides all this, there was generally a ridge or a furrow in the way wherever she wanted to send the hedgehog to, and, as the doubled-up soldiers were always getting up and walking off to other parts of the ground, Alice soon came to the conclusion that it was a very difficult game indeed.

The players all played at once without waiting for turns, quarrelling all the while, and fighting for the hedgehogs; and in a very short time the Queen was in a furious passion, and went stamping about, and shouting, 'Off with his head!' or 'Off with her head!' about once in a minute.

'I don't think they play at all fairly,' Alice said to herself, in rather a complaining tone, 'and they all quarrel so dreadfully one can't hear oneself speak – and they don't seem to have any rules in particular; at least, if there are, nobody attends to them – and it's so confusing all the things being alive; there's the arch I've got to go through next walking about at the other end of the ground – and I should have croqueted the Queen's hedgehog just now, only it ran away when it saw mine coming.'

*   *   *

Alice thought she might as well go back and see how the game was going on, so she went in search of her hedgehog.

The hedgehog was engaged in a fight with another hedgehog, which seemed to Alice an excellent opportunity for croqueting one of them with the other: the only difficulty was, that her flamingo was gone across to the other side of the garden, where Alice could see it trying in a helpless sort of way to fly up into one of the trees.

By the time she had caught the flamingo and brought it back, the fight was over, and both the hedgehogs were out of sight: 'but it doesn't matter much,' thought Alice, 'as all the arches are gone from this side of the ground.'

from *Alice's Adventures in Wonderland* by Lewis Carroll

* Alice finds everything about this game very confusing. At times, it is so strange that it may seem rather like a nightmare (although it may also make you laugh). Which parts of the extract, if any, do you find funny or nightmarish?

1. In the land which Alice is visiting, the animals talk as well as the people. What do you think the hedgehogs and flamingoes would have to say about this game of croquet? Write the conversations they might have amongst themselves after the game.

2. 'The players all played at once without waiting for turns, quarrelling all the while, and fighting for the hedgehogs.' Imagine what games such as golf or bowls would be like if everyone played at once without waiting for turns. Try to describe such a game as if you were a sports commentator.

3. Some games which seem ordinary and sensible to us, might appear very strange to a person from another country, or even from another time or planet. Try to describe a well-known game as a complete outsider might see it. Here, as an example, is one person's description of the game of cricket:

> You have two sides; one out in the field
> and one in.
> Each man that's in the side that's in goes
> out and when he's out he comes in and the next
> man goes in until he's out.
> When they are all out, the side that's out
> comes in and the side that's been in goes out
> and tries to get those coming in, out.
> Sometimes you get men still in and not out.
> When both sides have been in and out including
> the not-outs, that's the end of the game.
>
> *Marylebone Cricket Club*

Words

1. Below is a list of words connected with games and sports. The meanings of the words are given in the list on the right, but these are not in the same order as the words. See if you can find the correct meaning for each word.

1. game	a.	a game to decide a tie
2. tournament	b.	a struggle for victory
3. gala	c.	a formal contest or game
4. match	d.	an item in a programme of sports
5. event	e.	a series of games
6. championship	f.	one stage in a competition
7. play-off	g.	a trial of ability
8. competition	h.	a sport of any kind
9. round	i.	a contest to find the best player
10. contest	j.	a festivity

2. See if you can fit these ten words into the right spaces in the piece of writing below. Please do not write on this book: copy the piece of writing out or number your answers one to ten. You may have to change some of the words to their plural forms to make them fit.

The _____ began with a series of team _____. These included a swimming _____, and a football _____, which the previous year had ended in a draw so that a _____ had had to be held. There was also an individual knock-out _____, in which the winner of the final _____ was declared to have won the _____. At the end of the afternoon, a beauty _____ was held, which Karen insisted on entering, although we all warned her that she didn't stand a chance of winning. In spite of the cloudy weather, all the _____ were well supported.

Motsford: giving directions

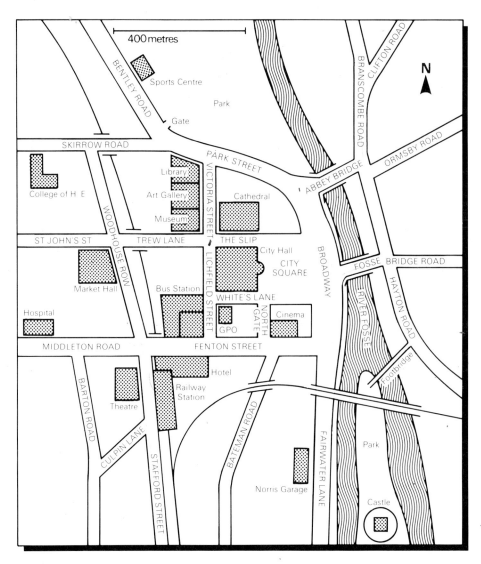

* Look at the map of Motsford town centre. Get used to the plan by asking your partner questions of this sort:

a. I come out of the Market Hall and turn right onto Woodhouse Row. I go along Woodhouse Row until I reach the crossroads where I turn left, crossing the bridge over the railway. I then take the second turning on the right and go under the railway line following the line of the river until I reach the first building shown on the map. Where am I?

b. I come out of the station and turn right onto Stafford Street. I take the third turning on the right, cross a railway bridge, and then take the first turning on the left. I enter the gate on the right. Where am I?

c. I come into the town from Clifton, cross the river at the first opportunity and then turn left. I take the first turning on the right and enter the first building on the right, shown on the map. Where am I?

d. I come out of the College of Higher Education and turn right onto Skirrow Road. I walk as far as the river and cross it using the second bridge I come to. Having crossed the river, I take the first turning on the right and walk along that road until I come to the footpath on the right. I follow the footpath, cross the river and turn left under the railway line. What building am I facing?

∗ Now, working with a partner, take turns to give one another precise directions on how to get from one place in the town to another, but do not tell your partner in advance what places you are sending him to. If your partner does not get to where you wanted to send him, try to find out why. Is it because your directions were poor or because he misunderstood them? Work at the problem until you can both give clear and accurate directions.

∗ Test your partner (and yourself) by asking several questions of that sort, then ask him more direct questions, for example:
   'How do I get from the hospital to the Ormsby Road?
             from the hotel to the sports centre?
             from Skirrow Road to Bateman Road?
             from the library to the theatre?'

1. You live in Clifton. Some relatives have been staying with you and are leaving from Motsford Station later today. On the way to catch their train they want to look at the city hall and the castle, and they have kindly agreed to return a book to the library for you. They also want to visit another member of the family who is a patient in the hospital. The bus from Clifton will drop them at Abbey Bridge.
    As you cannot go with them, write down directions for them, putting the visits in a sensible order so that they do not have to walk further than is necessary.

2. You have some foreign pen friends coming to stay with you for a week in Motsford, in the summer term. For the first two days of their visit, you will be unable to entertain them, as you will still be at school.
    Make a list of several places in Motsford which you think they might like to visit, and write a guide for them which will give accurate directions on how to get from one place to another in the town.

LOOKING AFTER ANIMALS

Pets

* Do you keep a pet at home?

* If you do — what is it called?
- — how long have you had it?
- — what do you feed it?
- — how do you look after it?

* What is your favourite sort of pet?

* Have you ever kept an unusual pet or do you know anyone who has?

* If you wanted to keep a pet you knew very little about, how would you find out how to look after it?

* Are there any pets you would not want to keep? Why not?

Prepare a talk to give to the rest of the class on one of these subjects:

How to look after a particular animal.
How to treat a sick animal.
How to train a pet.
A day in the life of a . . .
The day the mice, gerbil, canary . . . got out.
Working animals (for example, guide dogs).
The day our dog, budgie, cat . . . got lost.

Hedgehogs

This description is taken from a book about caring for animals.

The male hedgehog is known as the boar, the female as the sow. The two sexes are alike except for the fact that the boar is slightly larger than the sow. Their average length is just over ten inches, including the short tail, and the usual weight ranges from one to two and a half pounds. All the upper part of the head and body is covered with spines, each about an inch long. These spines, which give the characteristic prickly appearance, are arranged in groups, surrounded with fur. Through a special muscle arrangement, the hedgehog can roll into a tight ball with spines erect when threatened. When the enemy retreats, foiled by the bristles, the animal relaxes and the spines fall backwards, lying almost flat.

Hedgehogs can run fairly quickly, but their usual pace is a slow, rolling walk. When they have to descend high walls or ditches they roll up into a ball and drop, landing safely on the extended prickles. They can also swim well.

They are not very long-lived animals, two to three years being the average length of life.

Hedgehogs feed on worms, slugs, beetles and other small insects, and will also eat mice and even the young of birds. In captivity they can be given bread and milk, of which they are inordinately fond, raw and cooked lean meat, and offal, and any worms, cockroaches or beetles you can catch.

Hedgehogs are nocturnal animals, rarely appearing before sunset, when they can be found nosing about hedges searching for beetles and slugs. Late in November or December they hide away and hibernate in a warm nest of dead leaves, or even a deserted wasps' nest. Unlike dormice, squirrels and other rodents, they do not store up food, but rely on their accumulated fat. During the winter they may lose a third of their weight. When warm April returns the little creatures awake and look for water; then begin their yearly search for food.

from *Animals as Friends And How To Keep Them*
by Margaret Shaw and James Fisher

* What is the main purpose of the hedgehog's spines?
* What other use does the hedgehog sometimes make of its spines?
* Why are the animals called **hedgehogs**, do you think?
* What does **nocturnal** mean?
* Why might it be cruel to wake a hedgehog which was hibernating?

1. Write a factual description — like the one above — of an animal which is sometimes kept as a pet. Illustrate your description with sketches and diagrams where you think they are necessary.

2. Here is a part of a table giving advice on how to avoid being cruel to a pet, in this case, a cat.

Cats	
Things not to do	**Why not**
Don't keep the animal indoors all the time.	It will become lazy and inactive because of lack of exercise.
Don't forcibly wash your cat.	Cats keep themselves clean. They dislike being washed and may become distressed and over excited. If your cat does become very dirty, brush its coat clean when it is dry.
Don't handle the animal roughly.	It will become frightened and eventually may become nervous about being handled at all.

Discuss the advice given in the table above with someone else in the class, and see if you can add to it.

3. Choose an animal which can be kept as a pet and write an article giving advice on how to look after the animal. In your article include a table of things not to do.

Pain-Killer

Here is an extract from the book Tom Sawyer. *Tom Sawyer's Aunt Polly, worried by Tom's lack of energy and general low spirits, has taken to giving him a very unpleasant medicine called 'Pain-Killer'. Tom tries to think of ways to avoid drinking it.*

So he thought over various plans for relief, and finally hit upon that of professing to be fond of Pain-killer. He asked for it so often that he became a nuisance, and his aunt ended by telling him to help himself and quit bothering her. However, she watched the bottle clandestinely.[1] She found that the medicine did really diminish, but it did not occur to her that the boy was mending the health of a crack in the sitting room floor with it.

One day Tom was in the act of dosing the crack when his aunt's yellow cat came along, purring, eyeing the teaspoon avariciously,[2] and begging for a taste. Tom said:

'Don't ask for it unless you want it, Peter.'

But Peter signified that he did want it.

'You better make sure.'

Peter was sure.

'Now you've asked for it, and I'll give it to you, because there ain't anything mean about *me*; but if you find you don't like it you mustn't blame anybody but your own self.'

Peter was agreeable, so Tom pried his mouth open and poured down the Pain-killer. Peter sprang a couple of yards into the air, and then delivered a war-whoop and set off round and round the room, banging against furniture, upsetting flower-pots, and making general havoc. Next he rose on his hind feet and pranced around, in a frenzy of enjoyment, with his head over his shoulder and his voice proclaiming his unappeasable happiness. Then he went tearing around the house again, spreading chaos and destruction in his path. Aunt Polly entered in time to see him throw a few double somersaults, deliver a final mighty hurrah, and sail through the open window, carrying the rest of the flower-pots with him. The old lady stood petrified with astonishment, peering over her glasses; Tom lay on the floor, expiring with laughter.

'Tom, what on earth ails that cat?'

'*I* don't know, Aunt,' gasped the boy.

'Why, I never seen anything like it. What *did* make him act so?'

''Deed I don't know, Aunt Polly; cats always act so when they're having a good time.'

'They do, do they?' There was something in the tone that made Tom apprehensive.[3]

'Yes'm. That is, I believe they do.'

'You *do*?'

'Yes'm.'

The old lady was bending down, Tom watching with interest emphasised by anxiety. Too late he divined her 'drift'. The handle of the tell-tale teaspoon was visible under the bed-valance. Aunt Polly took it, held it up. Tom winced, and dropped his eyes. Aunt Polly raised him by the usual handle – his ear – and cracked his head soundly with her thimble.

'Now, sir, what did you want to treat that poor dumb beast so for?'

'I done it out of pity for him – because he hadn't any aunt.'

'Hadn't any aunt – you numbskull. What has that got to do with it?'

'Heaps. Because if he'd a had one she'd a burnt him out herself! She'd a roasted his bowels out of him 'thout any more feeling than if he was a human!'

Aunt Polly felt a sudden pang of remorse. This was putting the thing in a new light; what was cruelty to a cat *might* be cruelty to a boy too. She began to soften: she felt sorry. Her eyes watered a little, and she put her hand on Tom's head and said gently:

'I was meaning for the best, Tom. And, Tom, it *did* do you good.'

'I know you was meaning for the best, Aunty, and so was I with Peter. It done *him* good too. I never seen him get around so nice –'

'Oh, go 'long with you, Tom, before you aggravate me again. And you try and see if you can't be a good boy for once, and you needn't take any more medicine.'

from *Tom Sawyer* by Mark Twain

¹*secretly*   ²*greedily*   ³*uneasy*

* What does Tom usually do with the medicine his aunt thinks he is drinking?

* Have a close look at Tom's 'conversation' with the cat before he gives it the 'Pain-killer'. How fair is he to the cat? Why do you think he holds this 'conversation'?

* The way the cat leaps around the room is described in such a way as to make us laugh, just as we might laugh at a similar incident in a cartoon film. Are we being cruel to laugh at the cat's antics?

* Is Tom unnecessarily cruel to the cat?

* 'What was cruelty to a cat might be cruelty to a boy too.' Do you think there are occasions when we do things to people which would be thought cruel if we did them to animals?

* Why does Aunt Polly decide not to continue giving Tom the medicine and not to punish him for his treatment of the cat?

1. People often hold one-sided 'conversations' with their pets, as Tom does with Peter the cat. Write the 'conversations' that might take place in some of the situations described below:

> a zoo-keeper feeding seals or sea-lions;
> someone watching a cat eating its food and then washing itself;
> someone exercising a dog;
> someone trying to catch a gerbil or a similar animal, which is hiding somewhere;
> someone trying to pick up an excited or frightened rabbit;
> someone comforting a pet which he or she has just rescued from danger.

2. Take one of the situations described above and write down the animal's thoughts as he or she is being spoken to.

Miss Peckerlea

Mr and Mrs Turner and their son Jimmy are visited one evening by a neighbour, Miss Peckerlea. Jimmy and his father are playing dominoes.

Mr Turner went and opened the door. 'Miss Peckerlea, what a pleasant surprise!' exclaimed Mr Turner. 'Come in.'

Miss Peckerlea came in. She was a thin lady with a fussy manner. She seemed to be sorry for everything. 'Oh, I'm sorry to disturb you,' she said. 'I'm sorry to come in so late. I expected Jimmy would be in bed.'

'Yes, it's long past his bedtime,' said Mr Turner.

'Will you have a cup of cocoa?' said Mrs Turner.

'I'm afraid I can't stay,' said Miss Peckerlea. 'It's Timothy, you see, he does worry so when I go out.' Then she looked at Jimmy. 'I'm afraid I'm disturbing your son's game,' she added.

'Not at all,' said Mr Turner. He turned to Jimmy. 'Stand up, will you, and say hello to Miss Peckerlea.'

Jimmy stood up. 'Hello,' he said.

'Hello, Jimmy,' said Miss Peckerlea. Then she addressed herself again to Mr Turner. 'I'm afraid I'm going to put you to some trouble –' she began.

'If everybody was as much trouble as you, Miss Peckerlea,' he said, 'this world would not be what it is.'

'Well, that's very nice of you to say it,' she said. Then she looked at the three faces, and asked quickly: 'Do you think you could look after Timothy for me while I'm away?'

'You bet your life we can,' said Mr Turner. 'Your little Timothy will be as welcome as the flowers in May. Isn't that so, Gladys?'

'Of course it is. He'll be no trouble at all.'

'I'll bring his seed across,' Miss Peckerlea said, 'He eats only the best, you know. But what's worrying me is that he gets so lonely when I'm away.'

'He won't be lonely here,' said Mr Turner. 'Will he, young fellow m'lad?'

Jimmy didn't answer.

'Timothy,' said the woman defiantly, 'seems to live only for me. I've never in all my life seen another budgie like him. D'you know that I've only to go out shopping for an hour, and he's in a proper dudgeon when I get back! He gets in a regular sulk if ever I go to service on Sunday. As for the pictures – they're out of it. I never knew a budgie to want so much attention – and it always has to be me! I wouldn't dream of leaving him, only the train journey did him no good last year, and the sea air wasn't to his fancy either. He was in a proper state when I got back.'

'Don't you worry,' said Mr Turner, 'he'll get every attention here. That I can guarantee.'

'Thank you all very much,' she said. 'I can rest more content now. But if he should begin to fret will you wire me at once?'

'By all means, Miss Peckerlea.'

'Oh, thank you. And now I must be off to him. By the way, I'll be leaving next Monday morning, and I should be home the following Sunday tea-time – all being well. I'll bring him and his cage over first thing on Monday. Good night.'

'Good night, Miss Peckerlea.'

She gave Jimmy a glance as she went off and softly closed the door.

'Fancy,' remarked his mother, 'a woman makin' such a fuss over a little bird like that.'

'Now then, Gladys,' said her husband, 'her little Timothy means as much to her as our Jimmy means to us.'

'In that case,' said Mrs Turner, 'what's all the fuss about?'

'Hy, Dad,' put in Jimmy, 'sit down and pick up your dominoes.'

'Dominoes at this hour of the night!' exclaimed his father. 'Nay, nay, lad, it's long past your bed-time.'

from *Timothy* by Bill Naughton

* 'It's Timothy, you see, he does worry so when I go out.' Who or what did you think Timothy might be when you first read this? Why?

* Why does Miss Peckerlea speak **defiantly** when she says, 'Timothy seems to live only for me'?

* What sacrifices has Miss Peckerlea made for the sake of her pet? Are all the sacrifices she makes necessary? Do you think she minds making them?

* Why does Miss Peckerlea take so much trouble over a budgerigar?

* Why do you think the writer gave Miss Peckerlea that name?

* How would you describe her to a friend of yours?

Later on in the story, Jimmy lets the bird out of its cage. It is happy, flying around the room, but becomes over-excited and dies of a heart attack. If someone's pet died through illness or accident while you were looking after it because the owner was on holiday, how would you break the news to him or her?

1. Write a letter to the owner, explaining what has happened and offering as much comfort as you can.

2. Write or improvise the conversation that might take place between you and the owner when you next met.

The Meadow Mouse

1. In a shoe box stuffed in an old nylon stocking
   Sleeps the baby mouse I found in the meadow,
   Where he trembled and shook beneath a stick
   Till I caught him up by the tail and brought him in,
   Cradled in my hand,
   A little quaker, the whole body of him trembling,
   His absurd whiskers sticking out like a cartoon-mouse,
   His feet like small leaves,
   Little lizard-feet,
   Whitish and spread wide when he tried to struggle away,
   Wriggling like a miniscule puppy.

   Now he's eaten his three kinds of cheese and drunk from his
       bottle-cap watering-trough –
   So much he just lies in one corner,
   His tail curled under him, his belly big
   As his head; his bat-like ears
   Twitching, tilting toward the least sound.

   Do I imagine he no longer trembles
   When I come close to him?
   He seems no longer to tremble.

2. But this morning the shoe-box house on the back porch is empty.
   Where has he gone, my meadow mouse,
   My thumb of a child that nuzzled in my palm? –
   To run under the hawk's wing,   '
   Under the eye of the great owl watching from the elm-tree,
   To live by courtesy of the shrike, the snake, the tom-cat.

   I think of the nestling fallen into the deep grass,
   The turtle gasping in the dusty rubble of the highway,
   The paralytic stunned in the tub, and the water rising, –
   All things innocent, hapless, forsaken.

                                      Theodore Roethke

In *The Meadow Mouse*, Theodore Roethke is saddened by the loss of
the baby mouse he rescued and looked after. He realises that without
protection, it is likely to be killed.

1. Write your own story or poem about the loss of an animal and what the animal's keeper feels about it. It could be a story you make up or something which actually happened.

Hedgehog

Twitching the leaves just where the drainpipe clogs
In ivy leaves and mud, a purposeful
Creature at night about its business. Dogs
Fear his stiff seriousness. He chews away

At beetles, worms, slugs, frogs. Can kill a hen
With one snap of his jaws, can taunt a snake
To death on muscled spines. Old countrymen
Tell tales of hedgehogs sucking a cow dry.

But this one, cramped by houses, fences, walls,
Must have slept here all winter in that heap
Of compost, or have inched by intervals
Through tidy gardens to this ivy bed.

And here, dim-eyed, but ears so sensitive
A voice within the house can make him freeze,
He scuffs the edge of danger; yet can live
Happily in our nights and absences.

A country creature, wary, quiet and shrewd,
He takes the milk we give him, when we're gone.
At night, our slamming voices must seem crude
To one who sits and waits for silence.

Anthony Thwaite

1. Make a list of the **facts** the poem gives us about hedgehogs. If the poet had simply wanted to inform us about hedgehogs, he would probably have written something more like the passage on page 101.
    What does each piece of information make you **feel** about the creature?

2. Choose an animal which you have observed closely and write a description of it; write a poem if you like. Try to show the reader what you feel about the animal, as well as describing its appearance and behaviour.

Animals in Captivity

* 'Zoos give us the chance to study animals closely and to discover more about their behaviour.'

* 'Zoos help to protect and preserve endangered species.'

* 'Zoos and circuses are fun.'

* 'Animals in captivity have a much more comfortable life than they would have in the wild; they are given regular food, and medical care, for example.'

* 'Zoos and circuses take great care of their animals; if they did not, the animals would soon sicken or stop performing well.'

* 'Wild animals kept in cages are no longer wild; they cannot behave naturally.'

* 'Making an animal perform tricks to amuse people is degrading.'

* 'It is cruel to take animals out of their natural environment.'

* 'Some people set up zoos or run circuses just to make money; the welfare of the animals is not their first concern.'

What do you think?

Words

We sometimes use the characteristics of particular animals to help us describe people or actions. We look at a ferret, for example, note that it is especially useful for searching out other creatures — like rabbits — down a burrow, and we use its name as a verb. So, **to ferret something out** means to search hard for something until we find it. Pigs are often thought of as greedy animals, and we can talk about someone **making a pig of himself** if he eats a great deal.

* Why do we use animals' names in these expressions?

  to have a whale of a time
  to take the lion's share
  to fox someone
  to make a monkey out of someone
  to wolf one's food
  to be dogged by bad luck
  to play cat and mouse with someone
  to be a snake in the grass
  to hog something
  to ape somebody

* What characteristics do you associate with the following animals?

flea	tortoise	eel
eagle	mouse	spider
elephant	hawk	octopus
ant	rat	parrot
butterfly	cheetah	snail
magpie	hippopotamus	duck
shark	giraffe	canary
crocodile	scorpion	badger

1. Can you think of ways of describing people or actions or things using some of these animals' names? For example, if you think of a shark as being vicious, you might write something like: **We were always frightened of our next-door neighbour; he could be vicious as a shark.** Or, if you think of a snail as being very slow-moving, you might write something like: **I wouldn't say he was slow on his feet, but I've seen snails run faster.**

Shapes and Angles

1. Take a pencil and some rough paper and follow these instructions:

  a. Draw a vertical line about two centimetres long.
  b. From the bottom of the vertical line, draw a horizontal line at right-angles to it, about one centimetre long, extending to the right.

What capital letter have you drawn?

2. Now try this example:

  a. Draw a vertical line about two centimetres long.
  b. From the top of the line, draw a horizontal line at right-angles to it, about one quarter of a centimetre long, extending to the right.
  c. Mark a dot half way down the vertical line and draw a horizontal line from it of the same length as, and parallel to, the line you drew in instruction 2b. above.
  d. Join the two right-hand ends of the horizontal lines with a semi-circle, which extends to the right of the vertical line.
  e. Mark a dot on a level with the bottom of the vertical line and about one centimetre to the right of it.
  f. Join the dot by a diagonal line to the centre dot you put on the vertical line in instruction 2c.

What capital letter have you drawn?

3. Now work in pairs. One of you give the other similar instructions to those above to draw a capital letter. Do not look at what your partner is doing until he has finished drawing the letter. If the letter he draws is not as you expected it to be, discuss what has gone wrong. Take it in turns to give instructions and to draw the letters.

4. Discuss with your partner the meanings of the following words and phrases. Search for them in a dictionary if necessary. When you are sure what each one means, draw small diagrams which will demonstrate this. Two examples are shown for you:

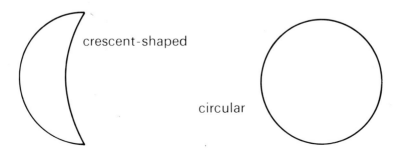

crescent-shaped

circular

square	vertical
rectangle/rectangular	horizontal
triangle/triangular	diagonal
circle/circular	symmetrical
semi-circle/semi-circular	hexagonal
crescent/crescent-shaped	elliptical
centre/central	opposite
axis	curved
	parallel

5. Now read the description below of a bird's eye view of an old village school and its surroundings, and draw it as accurately as you can.

At the village school, the bicycle shed lay opposite the back door. The shed was a tiny, square building and had just enough room for ten bicycles standing parallel to one another. In the centre of the back wall of the shed was a door which opened outwards onto a path.

The school playground, lying between this shed and the school, was also square, but about ten times bigger than the shed. It used to be divided equally by a wooden fence, and the marks where the fence posts used to be were still visible. When they left the school by the back door, the girls used to go left to their half and the boys right to theirs. At the corners of the yard were benches fixed into the ground, and these were placed diagonally opposite one another.

6. Below is the plan of a small park near the centre of a town. Study the plan, and then write a description of the lay-out of the park, making sure that the size, shape and position of each feature is clear.

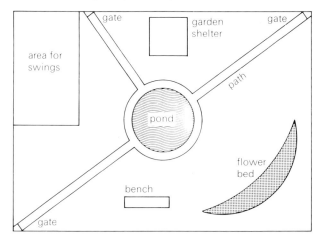

Paragraphs

Read these directions:

> To make one pint of milk for cooking purposes, add a measured pint of water to approximately 55 grams (5 heaped tablespoons) of dried milk. Once dried milk has been mixed, it may be boiled if it is heated slowly. With coffee or tea, allow the drink to cool to a little below boiling and add one or two teaspoons of dried milk.

Now read the same directions, put into paragraphs:

> To make one pint of milk for cooking purposes, add a measured pint of water to approximately 55 grams (5 heaped tablespoons) of dried milk.
>
> Once dried milk has been mixed, it may be boiled if it is heated slowly.
>
> With coffee or tea, allow the drink to cool to a little below boiling and add one or two teaspoons of dried milk.

The second set of directions is easier to read and understand because it has been arranged on the page in paragraphs. This helps the reader to pause at the end of each direction and think about what he has read.

The division between one paragraph and the next has been made so that each complete direction is separated from the others. The first paragraph tells you how to make a pint of milk; the second gives you advice on how to use it; the third paragraph tells you how to use dried milk in coffee or tea.

Most writing is divided up into paragraphs. As in the example above, this may be done to help the reader to pause and think, and it may be done to allow the writer to show that he is beginning a new section or aspect of his subject.

Paragraphs also make the pages of a book look attractive.

The writer shows he is beginning a new paragraph by starting to write about two centimetres in from the margin of the page. This is called **indenting**. In many **printed** books, the **first** paragraph of a piece of writing is not indented.

Here is a piece of writing taken from a story. It has been set out here without paragraphs:

> It was a surprise to both Karen and Paul, when they left the youth club, to find that the mist of the early evening had turned into a thick, choking fog. Paul took a few steps forward and immediately disappeared from view. Karen called to him to wait for her. He didn't need asking twice; he had to admit, if only to himself, that he was more than a little scared. He waited for Karen to reach him. It was comforting to know that he was not alone. They walked forward together, slowly, tentatively feeling with their feet for the edges of pavements; peering with half-blinded eyes to make out familiar corners and landmarks. Everything seemed distorted. Even their voices sounded muffled as though surrounded by swathes of thick felt. They crept along, yard by yard, feeling their way by the touch of walls and hedges. It was just as they turned the corner of their own street that Karen stumbled over something lying across the pavement.

The piece of writing above should be set out in paragraphs.

1. Decide with a partner where you think the divisions should be made.

2. Compare your ideas with what other groups have suggested, and try to give reasons to support your decisions. There may be several good ways of setting out this piece, but you should accept only sensible divisions. Look back at the earlier statements about paragraphs to help you discuss which ideas to accept and which to reject.

Here is an item of news taken from *The Star* of 6 November 1805. The editor of the newspaper obviously decided that it should be printed as a single paragraph. A news editor today would almost certainly print it divided into more than one.

1. Decide where you would make the divisions.

2. Compare your suggestions with those of other members of the class.

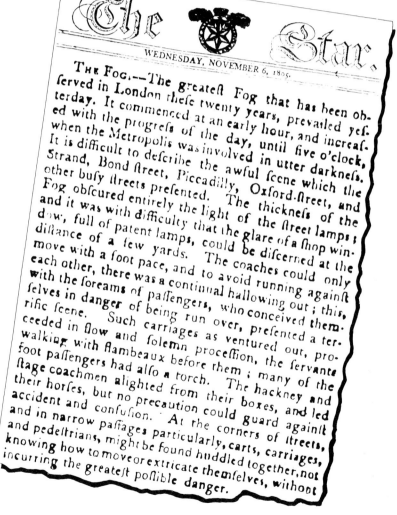

The Star

WEDNESDAY, NOVEMBER 6, 1805.

THE FOG.—The greatest Fog that has been observed in London these twenty years, prevailed yesterday. It commenced at an early hour, and increased with the progress of the day, until five o'clock, when the Metropolis was involved in utter darkness. It is difficult to describe the awful scene which the Strand, Bond street, Piccadilly, Oxford-street, and other busy streets presented. The thickness of the Fog obscured entirely the light of the street lamps; and it was with difficulty that the glare of a shop window, full of patent lamps, could be discerned at the distance of a few yards. The coaches could only move with a foot pace, and to avoid running against each other, there was a continual hallowing out; this, with the screams of passengers, who conceived themselves in danger of being run over, presented a terrific scene. Such carriages as ventured out, proceeded in slow and solemn procession, the servants walking with flambeaux before them; many of the foot passengers had also a torch. The hackney and stage coachmen alighted from their boxes, and led their horses, but no precaution could guard against accident and confusion. At the corners of streets, and in narrow passages particularly, carts, carriages, and pedestrians, might be found huddled together, not knowing how to move or extricate themselves, without incurring the greatest possible danger.

Setting out a Play

Read the short story below.

The Scratch

Elizabeth was doing her homework at the kitchen table when her mother came in.

'Liz,' said her mother, 'don't spread your stuff all over the table now. I've got to get the meal ready.'

'All right, Mum, keep your hair on,' said Elizabeth. 'I won't be a minute.'

'Get it cleared now!' Mother crossed the kitchen and began to lay the table.

'Oh, Mum, give me a chance,' Elizabeth grumbled.

'And while we're at it, I've got a bone to pick with you,' said Mother. 'I've told you about leaving your bike at the side of the house. If your dad catches the car on it again, there'll be real trouble.'

'I forgot,' said Elizabeth.

'Forgot!' said Mother, sarcastically. 'Go and move it now.'

'It's not fair!' said Elizabeth.

'And I thought you said you were going to mow the lawn.'

'I forgot.'

'Yes. Well, I've had to do it myself now. Just get those books out of the way and go and move that bike.'

At that moment the back door slammed, and Father's angry footsteps could be heard coming towards the kitchen.

'If your father's scratched that car. . .' said Mother.

'It's always *my* fault. Why can't he learn to drive properly?' shouted Elizabeth.

Father stormed into the kitchen.

'Who left that stupid lawn mower out?' he shouted. 'There's a scratch all the way down the side of the car!' He glared at his daughter. 'Elizabeth?'

'Oh,' said Mother. 'Would you like a cup of tea, dear?'

This story has been re-written as a play, on the next page. The words spoken by the characters in the story have not been changed, but there are several important differences in the way the writing is set out.

The Scratch

(Elizabeth is sitting at the kitchen table doing her
homework.
Enter Mother.)

Mother:	Liz, don't spread your stuff all over the table now. I've got to get the meal ready.
Elizabeth:	All right, Mum, keep your hair on. I won't be a minute.
Mother:	Get it cleared now!

(Mother crosses the kitchen and begins to lay the table.)

Elizabeth:	Oh, Mum, give me a chance.
Mother:	And while we're at it, I've got a bone to pick with you. I've told you about leaving your bike at the side of the house. If your dad catches the car on it again, there'll be real trouble.
Elizabeth:	I forgot.
Mother:	(sarcastically) Forgot! Go and move it now.
Elizabeth:	It's not fair!
Mother:	And I thought you said you were going to mow the lawn.
Elizabeth:	I forgot.
Mother:	Yes. Well, I've had to do it myself now. Just get those books out of the way and go and move that bike.

(A door slams off-stage and heavy footsteps are heard
approaching.)

	If your father's scratched that car. . .
Elizabeth:	(shouting) It's always *my* fault. Why can't he learn to drive properly?

(Enter Father, angrily.)

Father:	(shouting) Who left that stupid lawn mower out? There's a scratch all the way down the side of the car!

(He glares at Elizabeth.)

	Elizabeth?
Mother:	Oh. Would you like a cup of tea, dear?

1. Working with someone else, make a list of the differences between
the story and the play.

2. When you have finished, compare your list with the list on the next
page.

Differences between the story and the play

In the story	In the play
Speech marks are used in the usual way for the words which each person speaks: 'I forgot,' said Elizabeth.	Each person's name is written at the left hand side of the page. The name is followed by a colon (:) , which separates it from what the person says. There are no speech marks: Elizabeth: I forgot.
The narrator tells the reader what has **already** happened, and so the story is written in the **past** tense: Mother **crossed** the kitchen and **began** to lay the table.	The stage directions tell the actor what to do **now**, and so they are written in the **present** tense: Mother **crosses** the kitchen and **begins** to lay the table.
The narrator tells the reader how something **was** said: 'Forgot!' said mother, sarcastically.	The stage direction tells the actor how something **should be** said if this is not obvious. This direction is put in brackets: Mother: (sarcastically) Forgot!

Notice that each speech in the play still begins on a new line, starts with a capital letter and ends with a final punctuation mark.

Parts of Speech

It is sometimes useful to be able to give labels to the words you write. These labels are known as their **parts of speech**. Five of these parts of speech are: article, noun, adjective, verb, adverb.

article: **the, a, an**
an article simply introduces a noun.

noun: a noun is the name of something: **table, house, man, nose, garden, dog**
    or a noun is the name of a particular person, place or thing: **Sarah, Mr McPherson, Ireland, London, Ford Fiesta, Concorde**
    or a noun is the name of a group of things: **tribe, fleet, shoal, flock**
    or a noun is the name of a feeling or quality: **hope, fear, cowardice, truth, love, happiness, surprise**

adjective: an adjective is a word which is added to a noun to describe or define it:
a **large** table
an **overgrown** garden
a **foolish** person
a **faint** hope
a **needless** worry

verb: a verb is a word which conveys action or makes a statement about something:
The dog **limped**.
You **are** happy.
The Land Rover **struck** a rock.
Michael **used to laugh**.
The bus **would not start**.
The judge **wants to know** the truth.

adverb: an adverb is a word which is added to a verb to show how, when or where something is done:
The car was driven away **furiously**.
The cat miaowed **feebly**.
They left the country **yesterday**.
Do it **now**.
It's not **here**.
Put the books down **somewhere**.

or   an adverb is a word which is added to an adjective to help describe something:
The injured man was **very** pale.
My pudding tasted **quite** disgusting.

or   an adverb is a word which is added to another adverb to help show how, when or where something is done:
The minutes dragged by **very** slowly.
He **nearly** always refused.

Here are some short sentences set out in columns. At the top of each column is the name of the part of speech of the words in that column.

article	adjective	noun	verb	adverb
The	huge	tree	swayed	sickeningly.
An	old	woman	was crying	quietly.
The	junior	choir	will sing	soon.
The	sharp	pain	came on	again.
The	last	bus	left	yesterday.
The	leading	car	turned	suddenly.
A	well-oiled	machine	should run	efficiently.
The	unknown	disease	spread	rapidly.

Of course, sentences are not always written in the order: article, adjective, noun, verb, adverb. Can you identify the parts of speech in the sentences below, some of which are written in a different order? Sometimes, the same part of speech will occur more than once in a sentence.

1. Slowly, the hot-air balloon left the ground.
2. Noisy crowds quickly filled the square.
3. The patients will not be able to leave the old hospital yet.
4. Now, visitors can enter the ancient tomb.
5. The show is probably going to be a terrible disaster.
6. Dirty boots must be taken off immediately.
7. The amateur orchestra played remarkably well.
8. A friendly smile always helps.
9. The river is frozen completely today.
10. Yesterday, Uncle Henry finally retired.

Syllables

The sounds which make up words are called syllables. A syllable is part of a word which can be sounded by itself.

These words have one syllable:

breath	coat
cow	tap

These words have two syllables:

trousers	splinter
turnip	garage

These words have three syllables:

lemonade	ambulance
bicycle	telephone

These words have four syllables:

supermarket	comprehensive
television	agriculture

How many syllables are there in your name? How many syllables are there in your friends' names?

1. Here are twenty words. Sort them out into groups, putting all the words of one syllable into one group, all the words of two syllables into another group, and so on.

accident	unusual	school	fence	radiator
personality	circus	depart	marmalade	strength
motorway	refrigerator	manufacturer	giraffe	
probably	American	church	interrogation	
tin-opener	lesson			

To help you pronounce words correctly, the dictionary adds an accent mark or stroke after the syllable that is emphasised or stressed when a word is spoken.

Here is a list of words in which the stressed part of each word has been printed in bold type to help show how these stress marks work.

pur'pose	togeth'er
wo'man	referee'
beware'	registra'tion
li'brary	veg'etables
al'ligator	embar'rassment

uncharacterist'ically

2. Look again at the list of words in number 1 which you sorted into groups. Put in the stress mark to show which syllable is stressed when each word is spoken. If a word has only one syllable, the stress must be on the whole word, so a stress mark is not needed.

Using a Dictionary

A good dictionary will tell you:

1. how to spell a word correctly,
2. how to pronounce a word correctly,
3. what part of speech it is,
4. what the word means,
5. where the word comes from.

With this in mind, study this page from a dictionary carefully.

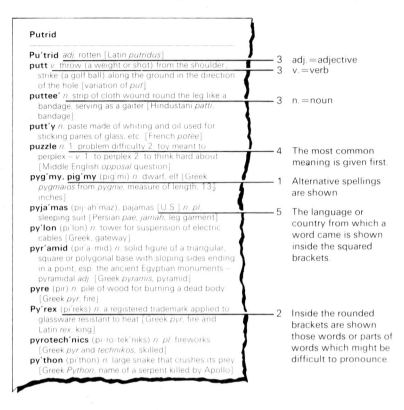

Putrid

Pu'trid *adj.* rotten [Latin *putridus*]
putt *v.* throw (a weight or shot) from the shoulder; strike (a golf ball) along the ground in the direction of the hole [variation of *put*]
puttee' *n.* strip of cloth wound round the leg like a bandage, serving as a gaiter [Hindustani *patti,* bandage]
putt'y *n.* paste made of whiting and oil used for sticking panes of glass, etc. [French *potée*]
puzzle *n.* 1. problem difficulty 2. toy meant to perplex — *v.* 1. to perplex 2. to think hard about [Middle English *opposal* question]
pyg'my, pig'my (pig'mi) *n.* dwarf, elf [Greek *pygmaios* from *pygme,* measure of length, $13\frac{1}{2}$ inches]
pyja'mas (pij-ah'maz), pajamas [U.S.] *n. pl.* sleeping suit [Persian *pae, jamah,* leg garment]
py'lon (pi'lon) *n.* tower for suspension of electric cables [Greek, gateway]
pyr'amid (pir'a-mid) *n.* solid figure of a triangular, square or polygonal base with sloping sides ending in a point, esp. the ancient Egyptian monuments — pyramidal *adj.* [Greek *pyramis,* pyramid]
pyre (pir) *n.* pile of wood for burning a dead body [Greek *pyr,* fire]
Py'rex (pi'reks) *n.* a registered trademark applied to glassware resistant to heat [Greek *pyr,* fire and Latin *rex,* king]
pyrotech'nics (pi-ro-tek'niks) *n. pl.* fireworks [Greek *pyr* and *technikos,* skilled]
py'thon (pi'thon) *n.* large snake that crushes its prey [Greek *Python,* name of a serpent killed by Apollo]

— 3 adj. = adjective
— 3 v. = verb

— 3 n. = noun

— 4 The most common meaning is given first.

— 1 Alternative spellings are shown

— 5 The language or country from which a word came is shown inside the squared brackets.

— 2 Inside the rounded brackets are shown those words or parts of words which might be difficult to pronounce.

1. Working with someone else, see if you can agree on the correct way to pronounce each word from the dictionary extract.

2. From a dictionary, find out how to pronounce these words:

chaos   scimitar   plait   either   crescent   schedule
decision   psalm   gnu   psychic   naïve   posse

3. From a dictionary, find out what parts of speech these words are:

bask   magnificent   foolish   suddenly   hotel   now
breathe   breath   rotate   ignorant   soothe   lucky

4. From a dictionary, find out where these words come from:

matador   assassin   boycott   jersey   bungalow   iris
poncho   caftan   diesel   yacht   sleuth   bayonet

5. From a dictionary, find out the meanings of any of the words in the lists above which you have not come across before.

DRAGONS

In St Leonard's Forest

This description of a dragon is taken from a pamphlet published in 1614.

A true and wonderful discourse relating a
strange and monstrous Serpent (or Dragon)
lately discovered, and yet living, to the great
Annoyance and *divers* Slaughters of both   *several*
Men and *Cattell*, by his strong and violent   *farm animals*
Poison; in Sussex, two miles from *Horsam*,   *Horsham*
in a woode called St Leonard's Forrest, and
thirtie miles from London, this present
month of August, 1614. With the true
Generation of Serpents.   *breed*

   In Sussex, there is a pretty market-towne,
called Horsam, and neare unto it a forrest,
called St Leonard's Forrest, and there is an
unfrequented place, heathie, vaultie, full of
unwholesome shades, and overgrowne
hollowes, where this serpent is thought to be
bred; but, wheresoever bred, certaine and
too true it is, that there it yet lives. Within
three or four miles compasse are its usual
haunts, oftentimes at a place called Faygate,
and it hath been seen within half a mile of
Horsam; a wonder, no doubte, most terrible
and noisome to the inhabitants thereabouts.
There is always in his track or path left a
glutinous and slimie matter (as by a small
similitude we may perceive in a snail's)   *similarity*
which is very corrupt and offensive to the
scent. . . .

   This serpent (or dragon, as some call it) is
reputed to be nine feete, or rather more, in
length, and shaped almost in the form of an
axletree of a cart; a quantitie of thickness in   *wooden axle*
the middest, and somewhat smaller at both
endes. The former part, which he shootes
forth as a necke, is supposed to be an *elle*   *about one metre*
long; with a white ring, as it were, of scales
about it. The scales along his backe seem to
be blackish, and so much as is discovered
under his bellie, appeareth to be a red. . . .

It is likewise discovered to have large feete, but the eye may be there deceived; for some suppose that serpents have no feete. . . . He rids away (as we call it) as fast as a man can run. He is of countenance very proud, and at the sight or hearing of men or cattel, will raise his neck upright, and seem to listen and looke about, with great arrogancy. There are likewise upon either side of him discovered, two great bunches so big as a large foote-ball, and (as some think) will in time grow to wings; but God, I hope, will (to defend the poor people in the neighbourhood) that he shall be destroyed before he grow so *fledge*.

He will cast his venome about *four rodde* from him, as by woefull experience it was proved on the bodies of a man and a woman coming that way, who afterwards were found dead, being poysoned and very much swelled, but not prayed upon. Likewise a man going to chase it and, as he imagined, to destroy it with two mastive dogs, as yet not knowing the great danger of it, his dogs were both killed, and he himselfe glad to return withe haste to preserve his own life. Yet this is to be noted, that the dogs were not prayed upon, but slaine and left whole; for his food is thought to be, for the most part, in a *conie*-warren, which he much frequents. . . .

The persons, whose names are hereunder printed, have seene this serpent, besides divers others, as the carrier of Horsam, who lieth at the White Horse in Southwark, and who can certifie the truth of all that has been here related.

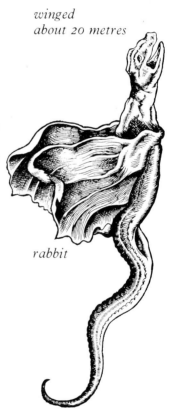

winged

about 20 metres

rabbit

John Steele
Christopher Holder
and a Widow Woman dwelling neare Faygate.

from *Folklore of Sussex* by J. Simpson

* Imagine you are walking in St Leonard's Forest and you catch a glimpse of this 'dragon' for a few seconds. It turns towards you, and so you run away. As you stumble out of the forest, you meet a friend and try to describe what you saw.

Without re-reading the account, describe what you saw to someone else in the class and try to answer any questions he or she asks about the creature which you saw. Your partner should try to ask at least five questions about what you saw, and you must attempt to answer these questions.

* With your partner, look back through the account and see how close your description was to the original.

* How can you explain any differences?

* One of the things which shows that this account was written over three hundred and fifty years ago is that the spelling of many of the words has changed. Find some examples of this.

What else about the account shows that it was written a long time ago? Think about the way the writers express themselves, as well as about what they say.

1. Below is a list of words from the account. Find where they appear and, using a dictionary if necessary, suggest some more familiar words or phrases which could replace them:

discourse	vaultie	venome
relating	compasse	woefull
yet	noisome	slaine
slaughters	countenance	lieth

2. Make a list of the facts about the dragon which are reported in the account. For example:

It is at least nine feet long.
It wanders within three or four miles radius of the forest.

3. Imagine you are the mayor of Horsham or a leading citizen of the town and you wish to collect more information about the creature. Design a poster to be pinned up around the town asking for people to come forward if they know anything about the creature. The poster should include a labelled drawing of the dragon, based on the information in your list, and details of any important facts about it that are not shown in the drawing.

* Read aloud the first two paragraphs of the account. Which of the paragraphs sounds more 'official' or formal, like an announcement?

Which one tries to give the listener a sense of tho atmoophere of the place and the unpleasantness of the creature?

Working with someone else, try reading each paragraph in as many different tones of voice as you can think of. Can you agree on which tone of voice suits each paragraph best?

4. Design and write a pamphlet to warn people of the possible dangers from the creature and giving them two pieces of advice:

    a. how to avoid being killed or injured if they meet the creature.

    b. what to do in order to protect themselves and their families, their homes and their animals from attack by the creature.

5. Many people in the town want the dragon to be killed as soon as possible; others want the chance to study it and learn more about it. A meeting is called to decide what is to be done. Either write a speech to persuade people to destroy the creature, or write a speech to persuade them to spare it so that the creature and its habits can be studied.

6. Nowadays there are few, if any, reports of sightings of dragons or serpents, but mysteries like the Loch Ness monster and unidentified flying objects (UFOs) attract a lot of interest. Like John Steele and his friends who signed the report about the dragon in St Leonard's Forest, many people send reports to the press and the police, testifying that they have seen unidentified flying objects and describing them in similar detail.

Look at the picture on the following page. Imagine you have seen an unidentified flying object. Write the report you would send to the press or the police, describing what you saw and where you saw it in as much detail as possible.

Knucker

This story about the killing of a dragon near Lyminster in Sussex, was told to a man called Charles Joiner in 1929 by a man from Toddington, who was trimming a hedge near Knucker Hole, a deep pool fed by an underground stream.

Knucker, said the hedger, was a great dragon who lived in the pool 'dunnamany[1] years ago'. Not only would he snap up cows, horses and men for his supper, but he would go swimming in the river Arun 'sticking his ugly face up agin the winders in Shipyard when people was sitting having their tea', till the Mayor of Arundel offered a large reward to anyone who would put an end to the Knucker.

So this Jim Puttock, he goes to Mayor and tells him his plan. And Mayor he says everybody must give 'en what he asks, and never mind the expense, 'cause they oughter be thankful anyway for getting rid of the Knucker.

So he goes to the smith and horders a gert iron pot – 'bout *so* big. And he goes to the miller and asks him for so much flour. And he goes to the woodman and tells 'en to build a gert stack-fire in the middle of the square. And when 'twas done, he set to and made the biggest pudden that was ever seen.

And when 'twas done · not that 'twas quite done – bit sad in the middle, I reckon, but that was all the better, like – they heaved 'en onto a timber-tug,[2] and somebody lent 'en a team to draw it, and off he goes, bold as a lion.

All the people follow 'en as far as the bridge, but they dursn't goo no furder, for there was ole Knucker, lying just below Bill Dawes's. Least, his head was, but his neck and body-parts lay all along up the hill, past the station, and he was a-tearing up the trees in Batworth Park with his tail.

And he sees thisyer tug a-coming, and he sings out, affable-like, 'How do, Man?'

'How do, Dragon?' says Jim.

'What you got there?' says Dragon, sniffing.

'Pudden,' says Jim.

'Pudden?' says Dragon. 'What be that?'

'Just you try,' says Jim.

And he didn't want no more telling – pudden, horses, tug, they were gone in a blink. Jimmy 'ud 'a gone too, only he hung on to one of they trees what blew down last year.

'Tweren't bad,' says Knucker, licking his lips.

'Like another?' says Jim.

'Shouldn't mind,' says he.

'Right,' says Jim. 'Bring 'ee one 'sarternoon.' But he knew better'n that, surelye.

Fore long, they hears 'en rowling about and roaring and bellering fit to bust hisself. And as he rowls, he chucks up gert clods, big as houses, and trees and stones and all manner, he did lash so with his tail. But that Jim Puttock, he weren't afeared, not he. He took a gallon or so with his dinner, and goes off to have a look at 'en.

When he sees 'en coming, ole Knucker roars out: 'Don't you dare bring me no more o' that 'ere pudden, young marn!'

'Why?' says Jim. 'What's matter?'

'Collywobbles,' says Dragon. 'It do set so heavy on me I can't stand up, nohows in the wurreld.'

'Shouldn't bolt it so, says Jim, 'but never mind, I got a pill here, soon cure that.'

'Where?' says Knucker.

'Here,' says Jim, and he ups with an axe he'd hid behind his back, and cuts off his head.

That's all. But if you goos through that liddle gate there into the churchyard, you'll see Jim's grave.

from *Folklore of Sussex* by J. Simpson

¹*I don't know how many*   ²*cart for carrying tree trunks*

* With a partner, try reading the story aloud in as many different accents as you can. Which accent do you think best suits the story?

* How can you tell that someone is telling this story, not writing it down? Make a list of words and phrases from the story which show this.

* Like the report in *In St Leonard's Forest* on page 126, this is the story of the sighting of a dragon, but the two stories are very different in tone. The dragon in *In St Leonard's Forest* seems a very serious matter right from the start; Knucker seems an amusing dragon, almost a joke. What is there about *Knucker* which tells us — even in the first paragraph — that the story is not to be taken too seriously?

∗ The story-teller in *Knucker* does not describe the dragon itself in any detail, only what it did. What things does he give more details about? How does this help to make the story sound convincing?

∗ The last sentence of *Knucker* is put in by the story-teller to show that his story about the dragon is true. Does it do so?

∗ Here are six statements about *Knucker.* You may think that most or all of them have some truth in them, but that none of them is the whole truth. Discuss which one comes nearest to your feelings about the dragon and what you know about it from the story:

   a. People should have talked to the dragon and tried to understand it.
   b. It was a fearsome, horrible creature, and needed to be destroyed.
   c. It was a nice, friendly dragon and should have been left alone.
   d. It was a revolting beast, slimy and violent.
   e. It wasn't as bad as people made it out to be.
   f. It hadn't done much harm; it was lonely and just wanted to make friends.

∗ What do you think about these statements about Jim Puttock?

   a. He was a great hero.
   b. He was a drunken show-off.
   c. The trick he played was unfair.
   d. He did everyone a good turn.
   e. He was very brave.
   f. He was cruel and a cheat.

1. Think of a tall story of your own. For example:

   The day Mr Dodd's sheep flew away.
   The time the train from London came off the rails and travelled all the way up Albert Street.
   The day Mrs Adamson hoovered up her daughter's guinea pigs, which were later found unhurt.
   The ship that sank and rose again with all safe on board.
   The day Mrs Hoskin's washing caught fire.

Tell the story to a friend, putting in as much detail as you can to make it sound convincing.

2. Write one of your tall stories down as if it had been told to you.

Welsh Incident

'But that was nothing to what things came out
From the sea-caves of Criccieth yonder.'
'What were they? Mermaids? dragons? ghosts?'
'Nothing at all of any things like that.'
'What were they, then?'
                              'All sorts of queer things,
Things never seen or heard or written about,
Very strange, un-Welsh, utterly peculiar
Things. Oh, solid enough they seemed to touch,
Had anyone dared it. Marvellous creation,
All various shapes and sizes, and no sizes,
All new, each perfectly unlike his neighbour,
Though all came moving slowly out together.'
'Describe just one of them.'
                              'I am unable.'
'What were their colours?'
                              'Mostly nameless colours,
Colours you'd like to see; but one was puce
Or perhaps more like crimson, but not purplish.
Some had no colour.'
                        'Tell me, had they legs?'
'Not a leg nor foot among them that I saw.'
'But did these things come out in any order?
What o'clock was it? What was the day of the week?
Who else was present? How was the weather?'
'I was coming to that. It was half-past three
On Easter Tuesday last. The sun was shining.
The Harlech Silver Band played *Marchog Jesu*
On thirty-seven shimmering instruments,
Collecting for Caernarvon's (Fever) Hospital Fund.
The populations of Pwllheli, Criccieth,
Portmadoc, Borth, Tremadoc, Penrhyndeudraeth,
Were all assembled. Criccieth's mayor addressed them
First in good Welsh and then in fluent English,
Twisting his fingers in his chain of office,
Welcoming the things. They came out on the sand,
Not keeping time to the band, moving seaward
Silently at a snail's pace. But at last
The most odd, indescribable thing of all,
Which hardly one man there could see for wonder,
Did something recognisably a something.'

'Well, what?'
          'It made a noise.'
                    'A frightening noise?'
'No, no.'
          'A musical noise? A noise of scuffling?'
'No, but a very loud, respectable noise –
Like groaning to oneself on Sunday morning
In Chapel, close before the second psalm.'
'What did the mayor do?'
                 'I was coming to that.'

Robert Graves

* The questioner is having great difficulty in trying to persuade the witness to be precise about what the 'things' looked like. It is obvious that the witness was **there** but what did he see?

1. Write an interview between a reporter and someone who claims to have seen a strange creature or object which he or she finds very difficult to describe, although he remembers the place and the other events very clearly. The 'thing' he saw might have been a dragon, an unidentified flying object, a sea-monster, a ghost-like thing . . .

2. Write a longer interview in which several people are asked about the same remarkable incident, but cannot agree on exactly what it was that they saw. You could have an 'expert' being interviewed as well, trying to suggest possible explanations for what happened.

The Fire Dragon

Here is an extract from a modern version of Beowulf, *a long Anglo-Saxon poem.* Beowulf, *a warrior, and much-loved ruler of his people, and now near the end of his life, is called upon to make one last effort for them : he must fight the Fire Dragon, which is harassing them.*
    Read the poem aloud.

Then the hero, stern under his gleaming helmet,
With his stout mailcoat and thick-plated shield,
Strode out to meet his foe. Toward the mound he moved,
The rock rampart cleft with arch of stone. Close by,
Strongly from the earth gushed out a stream, whose wash
Boiled to fury in the dragon's furnace breath,
Dropped to the steamy ground so scalding-fierce,
So hissing-hot that Beowulf could tread no farther.
He halted – in a loud voice he shouted his battle cry.
Then the dragon awoke. Crackling, he uncurled; like the clash
Of shield upon shield, he uncoiled his scaly length;
With thunderclapping sound he twisted through the arch,
Spitting flame. He blackened the rampart, he scorched
And burnt the grass, as round and round madly
He bounded upon the bruisèd ground. Then Beowulf,
Wreathed in smoke and fire, ran upon the dragon;
Shielded, brandishing his sword, he struck him mightily –
The keen edge bit on the scales and glanced aside,
But roused his dreadful wrath. Uprearing, he flapped
Wide his monstrous wings, fanning the blaze
Tenfold; like a forest fire, tree-ravenous, devouring
All in its path, he bore down on the pygmy king,
Till Beowulf, choked in that frenzy of smoke and flame,
Scarce could breathe . . . he stumbled . . . he gasped for air . . .

from *Beowulf the Warrior* by Ian Serraillier

1. At the end of this extract Beowulf suddenly appears to be very small alongside the dragon: he is described as 'the pygmy king. Earlier in the extract, however, the writer wants to show us how brave and forceful a hero Beowulf is. For example, he writes that Beowulf was 'stern under his gleaming helmet'.
    Make a list of other words or phrases in the extract which help to show Beowulf appearing and acting bravely and strongly.

2. Look again at the description of the dragon awakening:
'. . . Crackling, he uncurled; like the clash
Of shield upon shield, he uncoiled his scaly length;'
The sounds of words like **crackling** and **uncoiled** reflect their meaning.
   Make a list of other words in the extract whose sound is like their meaning.

3. The writer also likens the sound of the dragon's movement to the sound of shields clashing. Can you find another example in the extract of one thing being likened to another to help the reader to picture in his mind what is being described?

4. In the seventh line of the extract Ian Serraillier describes the water of the stream as 'scalding-fierce'. He has brought together with a hyphen two words which are not normally joined in this way in order to give the reader a strong feeling of what he is describing. Can you find other examples of this in the extract?

5. The poet often constructs his lines so that the full stop at the end of a sentence does not come at the end of a line, but near the middle of one. How many times does this happen in the extract? Why do you think the poet does this so often?

6. In each line of the poem three or four words have more weight than the rest. For example:
   'The **keen** edge **bit** on the scales and **glanced** aside'. The extra weight given to these words when the poem is read aloud gives it a clear, though irregular, rhythm.
   Re-read the poem aloud, experimenting with different rhythms until you think you have found the most effective way to read it.

7. Continue the story of Beowulf's fight with the fire dragon, as a poem if you wish.

The Monster

The mighty monster marched
Through silty, slimy swamp.
Fourteen feet a footstep,
With a clattering, crashing clomp.

His eerie but excellent eyes,
His terrible, tyrannous teeth,
Dribbled and dripped as he dashed
To the beautiful banquet beneath.

Maids and men were merrily munching
Bread, beef and beer of the best,
Unaware of the ugly, unwelcome,
Gate-crashing, gigantic guest.

Shouts and shrieks of shock,
Bellowing and beating of breasts,
As the monster munched the menu,
And greedily gobbled the guests.

Andrew Gosling

Idioms

Put your best foot forward
Put your nose to the grindstone
Toe the line
Bend over backwards to help
Put on a bold front
Stick your neck out
Stand up and be counted
Talk off the top of your head
Keep on your toes
Watch your step

If someone told you to try to do all the things suggested in the list above, and you took him **literally**, you would probably end up in hospital.

Such expressions are called **idioms**: they help to illustrate what we say by giving people a mental picture which suggests what we mean. For example, **to keep on your toes** suggests someone ready for action, like a boxer, and means to be alert.

Here are some more idioms, with their meanings, but in the wrong order. Can you sort them out?

1. To keep your nose clean

   To have a finger in every pie

   To stick your nose into something

   To turn a blind eye to something

   To chance your arm

   To turn a deaf ear to something

   To cut off your nose to spite your face.

   To have cold feet

   To pretend not to see

   To take a risk

   To do something that will harm you, out of spite

   Deliberately not to listen to someone

   To be afraid

   To interfere

   To keep out of trouble

   To be concerned in everything that is going on

? To have butterflies in your
   stomach

To do two jobs with one
   action

To send someone away with a
   flea in his ear

To lead a miserable existence

To lead a dog's life

To be anxious or
   apprehensive

To be a dog in a manger

To dismiss someone angrily

To buy a pig in a poke

To do things in the wrong
   order

To go on a wild goose chase

To begrudge someone the use
   of something which you
   don't yourself need

To kill two birds with one
   stone

To go on a very foolish errand

To put the cart before the horse

To buy something without
   first examining it

3. Read this conversation between two people:

First:	You look tired out.
Second:	I'm fed up!
First:	Oh, you won't want any cake then; I've just baked it.
Second:	I lead a dog's life!
First:	I might be able to find a bone somewhere . . .
Second:	It's driving me up the wall!
First:	Must be hard on the wallpaper, isn't it?
Second:	I'm at the end of my tether!
First:	Do you want me to untie it?
Second:	I'm all knotted up inside.
First:	I'm quite good at knots: I used to be in the Girl Guides . . .
Second:	I just had to talk to someone.
First:	That's right. (pause) Get it off your chest.
Second:	What? Are you trying to be funny?
First:	No, I meant —
Second:	What's wrong with my chest?
First:	Nothing. It's just a manner of speaking.
Second:	Not my idea of manners, making fun of people's chests.
First:	I didn't mean to be rude.
Second:	Well, just you mind your ps and qs in future.
First:	Pardon?
Second:	Just watch your step, that's my advice.

Write a conversation between two people in which they misunderstand one another because one or both of them takes idioms literally. The conversation might take place in a shop, or a hospital, or at school or anywhere you like.

Here is a list of some more idioms, which may help to give you ideas:

To look out for number one
To put the wind up someone
To pull the wool over someone's eyes
To take the rough with the smooth
To have your cake and eat it
To make someone laugh on the other side of his face
To be on your uppers
To be kept in the dark about something
To lead someone up the garden path
To look for the silver lining
To take pot luck
To have several irons in the fire
To be out of your depth
To show your teeth
To keep your head above water
To get the wrong end of the stick
To give someone the cold shoulder
To play to the gallery
To let sleeping dogs lie
To be down in the mouth

OPERATION OIL-FLOW

British minister for oil talks? Trade-dea

London (Wednesday): Mr
Minister for Energy, today
were about to begin between
Habib al Bakhti, of Saudiok
less, speculation continues
circles that a deal between the
would make sound economic
may need to import oil in the 19
is no doubt that Saudiokadi
return, value British know-how
bridge building, which Saudioka
needs in her programme of mode

In the House of Commons yes
Prime Minister refused to answer
from members of the Opp
'There is no time
of start
Opposition
talk

DATE	TIME OF ADMISSION	NAME	ADDRESS	NEXT OF KIN	INJURY	DOCTOR
27 Jan	11.32	Bektas Rachid	?	?	spine? haemorrhage	THS
"	11.32	James Davidson	12 Brandon Court London N1	Susan Davidson wife	spine?	THS
27 Jan	11.25	Sheikh Habib al Bakhti	Saudiokadia	?	shock/ lacerations contusions	BN
"	11.36	Frank Jennison	340 Spencwell Ave. London SE13	Lisa Jennison, wife	"	FN
"	11.35	Jim Clinson	YWCA Burgess Green London N4	George Clinson, Father	"	FN

SECRET ** SECRET ** SECRET ** SECRET ** SECRET ** SECRET ** SECRET

REDFORD DISTRICT HOSPITAL

Code: CRB/Gs/Oil-flow/256a

RESTRICTED ACCESS

Title: Operation Oil-flow, 27 January
information and time-table (Elverton Fields only)

PERSONNEL:

(Sheikh Habib al-Bakhti, Minister of Energy for Saudiokadia
Rachid, Private Secretary
Pilot

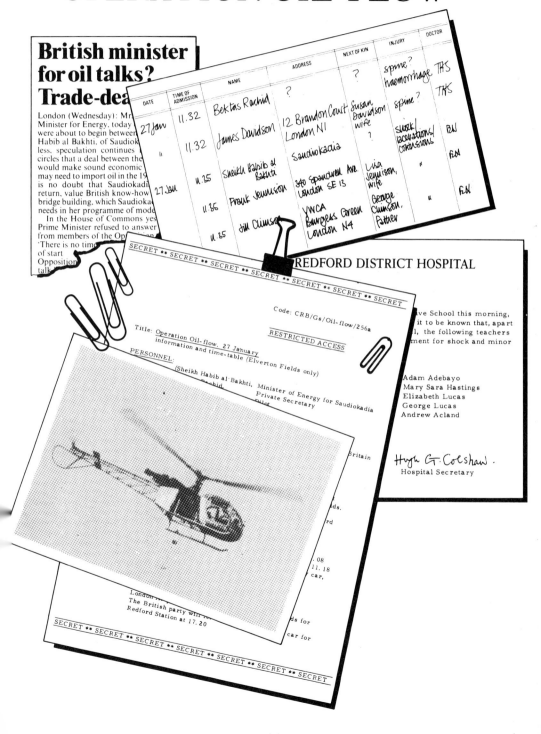

Britain

ds.
rd

.08
11.18
car,

London
The British party will re
Redford Station at 17.20

ds for

car for

ve School this morning,
it to be known that, apart
l, the following teachers
ment for shock and minor

Adam Adebayo
Mary Sara Hastings
Elizabeth Lucas
George Lucas
Andrew Acland

Hugh G. Colshaw.
Hospital Secretary

SECRET ** SECRET ** SECRET ** SECRET ** SECRET ** SECRET ** SECRET

Operation Oil-Flow

British minister for oil talks? Trade-deal hints

Article from Daily Gazette, 20 January

London (Wednesday): Mrs Grace Dignam, Minister for Energy, today denied that talks were about to begin between her and Sheikh Habib al Bakhti, of Saudiokadia. Nonetheless, speculation continues in government circles that a deal between the two countries would make sound economic sense. Britain may need to import oil in the 1990s and there is no doubt that Saudiokadia would, in return, value British know-how in road and bridge building, which Saudiokadia so badly needs in her programme of modernisation.

In the House of Commons yesterday the Prime Minister refused to answer questions from members of the Opposition. 'There is no tim[e]
of start
Opposition
talk[s]

SECRET ** SECRET ** SECRET ** SECRET ** SECRE[T]

Code: CRB/Gs/Oil-flow/256a

RESTRICTED ACCESS

Title: Operation Oil-flow, 27 January
information and time-table (Elverton Fields only)

PERSONNEL:

for Saudio-kadian Government	(Sheikh Habib al Bakhti,	Minister of Energy for Saudiokadia
	(Bektas Rachid,	Private Secretary
	(James Davidson,	Pilot
	(Frank Jennison,	Co-pilot
	(Jill Climson,	Stewardess
for British Government	(Mrs Grace Dignam,	Minister of Energy for Great Britain
	(Geoffrey Halton,	Permanent Private Secretary
	(Gordon Oakes,	Chauffeur/Bodyguard

MOVEMENTS:

The Saudiokadian deputation will travel by Concorde (British Airways) from Saudiokadia to London Airport (Heathrow), and thence by helicopter to Elverton Fields.
The British deputation will travel by car from Redford Station (BR).

TIMES:

Arrival
Mrs Dignam's party will arrive Elverton Fields 11.08
Sheikh Habib al Bakhti will arrive Elverton Fields 11.18
After formal greetings, both parties will travel by car, at 11.24, to Sellors Hall for private discussion.

Departure
Both groups will depart Sellors Hall for Elverton Fields at 17.00
Sheikh Habib al Bakhti will depart Elverton Fields for London Airport at 17.15
The British party will leave Elverton Fields by car for Redford Station at 17.20

SECRET ** SECRET ** SECRET ** SECRET

The account of Sally Laurence, English teacher

I have been asked to write down the events of the morning of 27 January as I experienced them:

Tuesday, 27 January was a bleak, cold day. The first two hours at school passed uneventfully until 11. 15 when I was teaching Form 1G in Room 15. This room looks onto the school playing-field. I was reading to my pupils from a novel when one of the boys suddenly blurted out:

"Miss, there's a helicopter!"

I was annoyed. He is a boy much given to disturbing the class. He enjoys getting attention. I told him quite sharply to be quiet and I continued to read. Within seconds a girl shouted:

"But it's crashing, Miss!"

I looked up, out of the window. The girl was right. The helicopter was crashing. I immediately shouted to all the children to get down onto the floor under their desks. Most did, but one or two evidently did not understand so I repeated the order and tried to duck my head under my table.

Just before I got quite underneath there was a very loud crash somewhere just outside the building, followed by a muffled explosion, then silence for a few seconds. Out of the silence I started to hear one or two quiet cries from some of the children.

There seemed to be a great deal of broken glass around the room, and some plaster had fallen off one of the walls or the ceiling, I'm not sure which. I could see that one of the children who had not taken proper cover immediately was now slumped in an awkward position across a desk. I started to move in that direction but must then have lost consciousness and I woke up in an ambulance on the way to the hospital in Redford, where I was treated for shock and cuts to the face, and then allowed to go home.

That is all I can remember about the incident.

Sally Laurence.

(Sally Laurence)

Extract from the Admissions Register, Redford District Hospital

DATE	TIME OF ADMISSION	NAME	ADDRESS	NEXT OF KIN	INJURY	DOCTOR
27 Jan	11.32	Bektas Rachid	?	?	spine? haemorrhage	THS
"	11.32	James Davidson	12 Brandon Court London N1	Susan Davidson wife	spine?	THS
27 Jan	11.35	Sheikh Habib al Bakuti	Saudi Arabia	?	shock/ lacerations/ contusions	BN
	11.35	Frank Jennison	340 Spandwell Ave. London SE 13	Lisa Jennison, wife	"	FN
	11.35	Jill Clunson	YWCA Burgess Green London N4	George Clunson, father	"	FN

REDFORD DISTRICT HOSPITAL

After the accident at Redford Comprehensive School this morning, the Hospital Management Committee wish it to be known that, apart from those five people detained in hospital, the following teachers and pupils were allowed home after treatment for shock and minor injuries:

Adults: Mr John Albert Curson
Miss Sally Laurence

Children: Kevin Graham Mitchell
Claire Hudson
David Manning
Kishor Patel
Hilary Booth

Adam Adebayo
Mary Sara Hastings
Elizabeth Lucas
George Lucas
Andrew Acland

No further bulletins will be issued.

Hugh G. Coleshaw.
Hospital Secretary

Bulletin issued to the press from Redford District Hospital, 27 January,

Ten Quick Questions

* Who is Mrs Grace Dignam?
* Where and when was she going to wait for the group from Saudiokadia?
* Why are the detailed arrangements for the meeting between Mrs Dignam and Sheikh Habib al Bakhti marked **Secret**?
* Where did Sheikh Habib al Bakhti and Mr Rachid board the helicopter?
* How many people were in the helicopter?
* At what time was the helicopter expected to reach Elverton Fields?
* What was happening in room 15 of Redford Comprehensive School as the helicopter was crashing?
* Which of the people in the helicopter was most seriously hurt?
* Why does the Admissions Register for the hospital have a column headed **next of kin**?
* What was the total number of people injured in the accident?

1. Working with a partner, act out one of these scenes:

   a. Two pupils in the English lesson just as the helicopter starts to come down near the school.
   b. Two pupils just after the crash; one of them has been injured.
   c. The school secretary just after the crash. She telephones the Emergency Services.
   d. A pupil describing what happened to a reporter, who is taking notes.
   e. Mrs Dignam and Mr Halton waiting at Elverton Fields as the helicopter is coming down to land.
   f. The pilot and co-pilot of the helicopter as it approaches Elverton Fields.
   g. One of the pupils, just arriving home telling his or her mother or father what happened.

When you have acted out one of these scenes, write it out in conversation form.

2. You are one of the pupils at Redford Comprehensive School. Both your parents are away from home, abroad on a visit. You are staying with your aunt and uncle for three weeks until they return. As soon as they hear the news about the helicopter crash, your parents telephone you to make sure that you are safe. International telephone calls are expensive, so, after reassuring them, you promise them you will send a long letter, saying what has happened. Write the letter.

3. Suppose you were injured in the crash and had to go to the hospital for a check. Write long entries in your diary for the day before the crash, then for the 27th, 28th, 29th and 30th January, 3rd and 10th February.

4. Write a newspaper report of the accident for your local newspaper. Include suitable headlines, for example:

HELICOPTER CRASHES AT SCHOOL
Amazing escapes for school children

Remember that people read newspapers for information, so your article should tell the reader:

WHAT	has happened
WHERE	it happened
WHEN	it happened
WHO	was involved

Your article may also tell **HOW** and **WHY** the accident happened, although you may not, at this stage of events, be able to give the correct reasons, and an article for a newspaper should report facts, **not** guesses.

Your article, apart from giving the answers to those questions, might also include pictures and interviews with people involved in the accident.

5. Draw a plan of the area where the helicopter crashed, showing its projected flight path to Elverton Fields; where it actually came down, and the damage it caused. Do not forget to put in the scale of the plan, and the compass directions.

6. The headmaster of your school would send a report about the accident to the Chief Education Officer of your county.
    Assume that you are the headmaster of your school, and write your report. Give a heading to your report (like a title):
Report Concerning Helicopter Crash at Redford School, 27th January.
Then state what happened, giving as much information as possible. The Education Officer would want to know such details as:

    a.   the number of injuries to pupils and staff, if any;
    b.   the amount of damage caused, in detail;
    c.   whether or not the school's safety precautions and fire-drill worked, and what could be done to improve them;
    d.   any recommendations that you, as headmaster, have to make as a result of the accident, about safety measures, routines, alterations to buildings, etc.

    Sign and date the Report.

Inventions

Look at this picture of the 'Eiffel Tower' bicycle, invented in 1894.

1. Working with a partner, make a note of any ways in which this machine might be better than an ordinary bicycle.

2. What are its disadvantages? Make a list of them.

3. How could the 'Eiffel Tower' bicycle be improved in order to remove some of its drawbacks without losing any of its advantages?

4. If these bicycles were in use now, what changes would have to be made to 'street furniture' such as traffic signs, road markings, traffic lights?

Look at this picture of Gauthier's monocycle, invented in 1877.

1. Make a drawing of the machine, looking directly from above it or from the front or rear of it. You do not need to include a rider in your drawing.

* How would the rider keep his balance?

* How easy would it be to start and stop?

* Would it be easy or difficult to turn corners?

* Would pedalling it be easy or hard work?

* Would it perform well in heavy traffic do you think?

* How would it perform on a hill?

* How would you get off the machine?

2. Working with a partner, make a list of the monocycle's good and bad points, as you did for the 'Eiffel Tower' bicycle.

3. You have been asked to make a test ride on one or both of these machines and to write a report for a cycling magazine. Write your report, explaining the problems and pleasures of your ride, starting from the moment you first look at the machine and get on it. Your report should include answers to the questions above.

4. Invent one of the machines listed below and draw labelled diagrams and sketches to show how it works.

    a ghost detector
    an automatic dog-trainer
    a fully automatic lawn-mower
    a device for straightening pigs' tails
    an underwater bicycle
    an automatic bed-maker
    a device for detecting and removing lumps in mashed potato
    a machine for shuffling playing cards efficiently and fairly
    a machine for detecting bad-tempered people
    a device for cutting one's toenails automatically
    an automatic tunnelling device
    a device for preparing and serving breakfast in bed
    an automatic slug exerciser
    a device to make eating spaghetti easier
    a machine for tossing coins completely fairly
    a device for delivering newspapers to houses where there are
        fierce dogs
    a device for removing insects and spiders from the house without
        killing them
    an automatic weed detector and hoe
    a device to cut up cream cakes or eclairs without squashing the
        cream out of the sides
    a device for assisting horse and pony riders into the saddle.

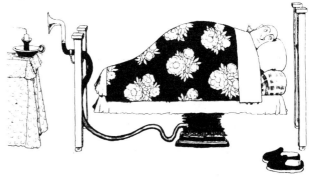

FRIENDS

Friends

I fear it's very wrong of me
And yet I must admit,
When someone offers friendship
I want the *whole* of it.
I don't want everybody else
To share my friends with me.
At least, I want *one* special one,
Who, indisputably,

Likes me much more than all the rest,
Who's always on my side,
Who never cares what others say,
Who lets me come and hide
Within his shadow, in his house –
It doesn't matter where –
Who lets me simply be myself
Who's always, *always* there.

Elizabeth Jennings

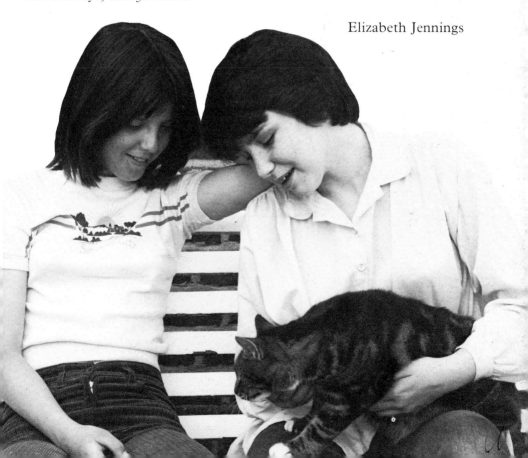

* Do you agree with what Elizabeth Jennings says she wants from a friend?

Is she being selfish?

Does she expect too much from a friend?

Why do you think she begins the poem by saying 'I fear it's very wrong of me'?

What do you think Elizabeth Jennings means when she says she wants a friend 'Who lets me simply be myself'?

* What do you think are the most important things about a friend?

1. Look at the statements below and re-write them in order of importance for **you**.

    a. I want a friend to stick up for me.
    b. I want a friend I can share a secret with.
    c. I want a friend who is fun to be with.
    d. I want a friend who doesn't get angry easily.
    e. I want a friend who likes the things I like.
    f. I want a friend who is popular with other people.
    g. I want a friend who will do what I want to do.
    h. I want a friend I can protect.
    i. I want a friend I can trust.
    j. I want a friend who looks up to me.
    k. I want a friend who will protect me.
    l. I want a friend who shares things.
    m. I want a friend to respect and follow.
    n. I want a friend who is kind.

* Compare your list with those made by other people and discuss the differences. Try to agree on some of the most important qualities you would look for in a friend.

2. Add other qualities to your list of things you look for in a friend which have not been mentioned in the list above.

Szolda

He was eleven and he'd been at school two months. His old man had been a university teacher, and he'd got in the school under some special rule, without having to take the exam. He wouldn't have got in any other way because his English was bad, worse than I'm putting it here. He was in the juniors and he didn't know anybody yet. But he knew me now. He made the most of that.

Because there was always the danger of the gang getting at him again, he started waiting for me to go to school, and again on the way back. I didn't mind. I didn't like him too much. But I didn't mind.

My mother saw him hanging about outside the house one morning.

'Is that boy waiting for you?'

'I suppose so.'

'Who is he?'

'I don't know, a Hungarian kid. He hangs around.'

'Is he called Szolda?'

'Yeah, something like that.'

'Get your nose out of that book at breakfast. And don't say "yeah". If you mean yes, say yes.'

'Yes,' I said, very distinctly.

'Is he a friend of yours?'

'No.'

'Try and be friendly to him. They're nice people. You know he's only got a mother, don't you?'

'Yeah. Yes,' I said.

'Well, remember she'll be making the same sacrifices for him that I am for you. Why don't you ask him in?'

I got up from the table fast. 'I'm going now,' I said.

'Have you got a handkerchief?'

'Yeah.'

'Not "yeah" – yes.'

The kid was leaning against the gate. He said brightly, 'Ready now, Woolcott?'

'*Yeah*,' I said, savagely.

He was all right. It was just that he had nothing to say. He didn't know anything about sport, and he didn't have a television. He just agreed with whatever you said. If you told him a joke, even a rotten one, he would laugh himself sick. If you said, 'Hold this', or 'Fetch that', or 'Run there', he would do it. It was like having a dog. My friend Nixon thought I was barmy to go with him. He said, 'Why don't you tell him to buzz off? There are plenty of juniors around.'

'He doesn't know any.'

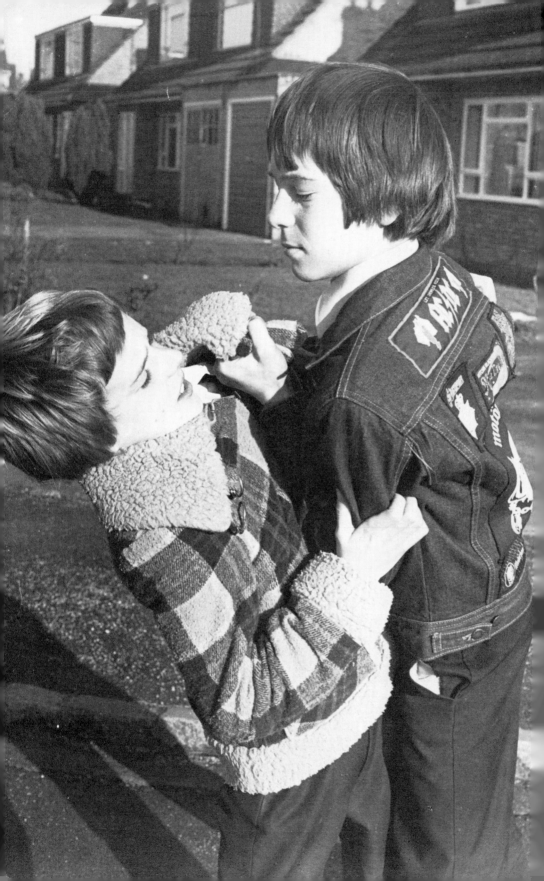

'That's his problem. We don't want him.'

'He's all right,' I said.

Nixon used to wait for me at the corner of Handley's Works, and one morning he was going on about last night's television. Every time I laughed and said, 'Yeah, wasn't it good?' the kid did the same. After a while this began to annoy Nixon.

'Why don't you shut up?' he said. 'I'm not talking to you.'

The kid didn't say anything.

'You haven't even got a television,' Nixon said.

The kid still didn't say anything. Nixon grew red in the face.

'Are you dumb or something?' he said.

I said, 'You just told him to shut up.'

'Then why does he laugh like a parrot when I'm talking to you?'

'I don't know,' I said.

'Then tell him to shut up. He hasn't even got a television.'

'Never mind about that.'

'Well, if he hasn't got one, he can shut up about it.'

'So can you.'

'So can I what?'

'Shut up about it.'

'Say that again,' Nixon said.

I said it again, and a minute later we were down on the ground. It was the first time we'd had a fight. He got his lip split and I got my trousers torn. He got up and went off.

The kid had been dancing around like a mad flea while this was going on and the minute I got up he started brushing me down.

I said, 'Just you leave me alone.'

'I'm sorry. I didn't want to cause trouble –'

'And shut up about it!' I said.

*　　　*　　　*

It was difficult having him around. Nixon and I made it up, but it was still difficult. Nixon's old man was a doctor and they were going to Norfolk for Christmas. His grandparents had a farm there. I was supposed to be going with them, but after our fight he didn't mention that any more. I was pretty sure he would mention it if I told the kid to buzz off.

Nixon was like that. If you wanted something you had to be pretty nice to him. If you borrowed his ruler or rode his bike you had to keep on about what a marvellous ruler it was or how it was the best bike in the world. It got a bit sickening after a while. He wasn't always like that. He had a good sense of humour and we had a lot of jokes that nobody else knew about. He was my best friend, really. But I still wouldn't tell the kid to buzz off because of him.

from *Run for Your Life* by David Line

* Why do you think Woolcott's mother wants him to be friends with Szolda?

* What would you feel about someone your parents told you you **ought** to be friends with?

* How do you know that Woolcott doesn't like the idea of inviting Szolda into the house? Why do you think he feels this way?

* When Szolda asks Woolcott if he is ready why does Woolcott say 'Yeah' **savagely**?

* When Szolda apologises for causing the fight, why does Woolcott tell him to shut up?

1. Make a list of the things about Szolda that might make him a good friend.

2. Make a list of the things which Woolcott finds irritating about Szolda.

* Szolda is obviously keen to be friends with Woolcott. What mistakes does he make in setting about the friendship?

* What is it about Woolcott that encourages Szolda to try to make friends with him? Would Woolcott make a good friend, do you think, from what you learn about him here?

3. 'He was my best friend, really'. Make a list of Nixon's good points; the things that make Woolcott want to keep him as a friend.

4. Make a list of Nixon's main faults, according to Woolcott.

* Why does Woolcott get into a fight with his best friend because of someone of whom he says, '**I didn't like him too much**'? Woolcott says about Nixon, '**I still wouldn't tell the kid to buzz off because of him.**' Why not?

* How does Woolcott know that his quarrel with Nixon is not entirely forgotten?

5. 'Nixon and I made it up, but it was still difficult.' Write the conversation between Woolcott and Nixon in which they try to patch up their quarrel.

6. Write a story in which two friends fall out because one of them has become friendly with a third person. The story could be based on experiences of your own.

Helping Out

Helen is an American girl. Her mother is ill in hospital a long way from home. While she is unwillingly weeding the front garden of her house she is visited by a friend – Betty – whom she has not seen for some time. Helen speaks :

'I thought you were at Quonset.'

'Well, I am. I mean, I was. Mummy had to come up for a day and she brought me with her. We came last night.'

'Why?' Helen couldn't imagine anyone leaving Quonset for even a day, and right now the thought of the cool, green waves and the delicious sound of the sea were almost too much to bear.

'I needed some new sandals and I had to go to the dentist. I told you I might. But that wasn't the real reason.'

Helen waited, but when Betty didn't explain, she had to ask.

'It's a secret just now,' Betty said and then she laughed. 'But I think you may know tomorrow.'

Helen was too hot and tired for secrets. It was wonderful to see Betty after having no one but Cindy to play with all summer. But Betty looked so happy and cool. She didn't have to work. She didn't have a mother who was ill. She didn't have any troubles at all. 'I don't care if I do know or don't know,' she said.

Betty saw how tired and hot Helen looked and she said quickly, 'I've got the rest of the morning before I have to go into town with Mother. Can I help?'

'No. You'll get all dirty.'

Helen was so glad to see Betty that she couldn't understand what made her cross. She wouldn't have blamed Betty if she had stamped and sulked and gone home the way Barbara Buckingham always did, but Betty only said, 'It doesn't matter if I do because this is a play dress. I've got to change it anyway. What are you doing – weeding?'

'Trying to,' Helen said, 'and I *must* get this bed done this week. It's the last one and when it's finished the garden will be all ready for when Mother comes home.'

'When's that?' Betty asked.

'She's going with Daddy to the White Mountains tomorrow to get strong and then she's coming back with him the Sunday before school starts – that's two weeks from the day after tomorrow.'

'I know because that's when we're coming home –.' Betty started to say something else and then changed it to, 'You know if you wet that bed with the hose, the weeds would come up a lot quicker.'

'I never thought of that,' Helen said, looking up at Betty with new respect.

'Well, let's.'

Helen and Betty worked together for the rest of the morning. As they worked, they talked, and by the time Auntie Chris rang the bell for lunch, they had forgotten that there was ever a time when they had not been close friends.

'I've got to dash,' Betty said, 'but, anyway, the old bed's done.'

Helen looked down and realised, for the first time, that what Betty said was quite true. There wasn't a spear of grass nor a dandelion head nor a single weed above the thick green of the lily-of-the-valley leaves.

Helen said, 'Can you come back this afternoon? We could swim in the mill pond, or play.'

'I can't. I've got to go into town right after lunch and then we're taking the four o'clock back to Quonset with Daddy.'

'Oh –' Helen looked down at her grubby hands and wished she could put the morning back again.

'But anyhow,' Betty said, 'the summer's almost over, and your mother's coming back.'

'Yes,' Helen said, but even now she didn't quite dare to believe it.

Betty ran off down the path, calling 'Good-bye' over her shoulder.

She doesn't really mind a bit, Helen thought. She's going back to her friends at the beach and I was just a filler-in for this morning. I hate her. I just hate her, she – but she knew she didn't hate Betty even for one moment, and she suddenly felt ashamed. She had never had a friend like Betty before, and even school would be different now. She picked up the tools and walked slowly to the back door.

from *The Funny Guy* by Grace Allen Hogarth

* Helen is irritable when Betty first arrives. How many reasons can you find that might have put Helen into a bad mood?

* Helen doesn't **want** to be rude to her friend. How does Betty show that she understands this?

* What qualities does Betty have that Helen's other friend, Barbara Buckingham, doesn't have?

* Look carefully at what Betty says and does. How does she help to re-start her friendship with Helen?

1. 'I just hate her, she – but she knew she didn't hate Betty even for one moment, and she suddenly felt ashamed.' Make a list of the reasons why Helen suddenly felt that she hated Betty. Why does she immediately feel ashamed of thinking that she hates Betty?

2. A new friend, whom you like very much, has called to see you. You are busy doing a job for your parents. You ask your friend to stay as you will soon have finished work and will then be free. Your friend refuses, having already promised to go to see someone else later. Continue the story of what happens, including the thoughts which go through your mind as you carry on working.

If you prefer, write the story as if it happened to someone else, not you.

3. Write the story of two people becoming friends.

4. Here are some more suggestions for writing about friends and friendships.

I am my own best friend.
Two's company, three's a crowd.
An unusual friendship.

* What is happening in the picture above? You do not know what is being said. How, then, can you tell what these people feel about one another and about what is going on?

What's in a Name?

Bernard lives in a Lancashire town and has three good friends, Maureen, Dougie and Terry. In this extract, his new Pakistani friend, Shofiq, is confirmed as a member of the gang.

The only confrontation, when Bernard had got them all together to tell them Shofiq was 'in', was over the word Paki. Even Bernard hadn't realised that Shofiq hated it – he'd even addressed his first note to 'The Paki' he recalled with a blush – and at first he'd been inclined to laugh at it. But Shofiq was serious.

'I can't rightly explain,' he said, 'but it's horrible. I mean I don't call you lot all Whities, or something. There's just something . . . it sounds . . .'

'Ah, rubbish, lad,' said Terry. 'Everyone calls Pakis Pakis. It stands to reason. I mean, my dad calls Pakis Pakis; and blackies. Like West Indian kids get called niggers and Chinese is Chinkies. I mean, it's just what you get called, it don't mean nowt.'

'It does, it does!' said Shofiq. 'I'll tell you, it means . . .'

He was helpless. He couldn't explain.

'I just wish you wouldn't, that's all,' he ended lamely.

'Rubbish!' said Terry firmly. 'I'll call you what I like, and you're a Paki, so there.'

Shofiq started to push up his sleeves.

'All right then, Smelly White Pig,' he said grimly. 'Take your coat off, lad, 'cause I'm going to batter you.'

Maureen solved it in the end by pointing out that no one was allowed to call Bernard Bernie. Bern was all right, or even Slobberchops, but not Bernie. They discussed as to why, but he couldn't rightly say. But he hated it, and that was that. Terry, who wasn't thick, agreed that he'd not call Shofiq a Paki.

'It's not just me, though,' said Shofiq. 'Everybody hates it, it's rotten. But thanks, Terry.'

'Well I won't call any of 'em – you – Pakis in future,' said Maureen. 'Pakistanis is good enough for me.'

Shofiq giggled: 'Or Indians, or Bangladeshis, or Sri Lankans, eh? How about British? It's on me birth certificate!'

But that just got them confused. In any case, Bernard wasn't too pleased with the way Maureen was making up to Shofiq. He was *his* mate. Anyway, perhaps she fancied him, and then he'd be jealous the other way maybe. So he started a good friendly punch-up to seal Shofiq's membership of the gang.

from *My Mate Shofiq* by Jan Needle

* The writer says, 'Maureen solved it in the end.' What was the problem and how did she solve it?

* Bernard 'started a good friendly punch-up to seal Shofiq's membership of the gang'. How can a fight show friendship?

* What does Bernard mean by 'then he'd be jealous the other way maybe'? What does this tell you about the way Bernard thinks of Maureen?

* Some people have nicknames and do not object to being called by them. Why does Shofiq object?

* Does it matter what we call people?

* People sometimes accept nicknames that are not very flattering – like Slobberchops. Why do people accept some nicknames and not others, do you think? Do they always have any choice?

1. Make a list of all the nicknames you know. Look at their lengths, their endings, their sound, and the number of syllables in each one. Can you work out what they mean and why they were made up? Can you see any similarities amongst them? How could you explain nicknames to someone who came from a place where they did not exist?

Canal Lock in Winter

They stood by the bank and called me names;
'Yaller,' they screamed and laughed like knives,
Pulled at their socks and blew their cheeks,
And pretended to split the ice with dives.

They thumbed their noses and gloated in dance,
And wagged their fore-nails with a sneer,
And guarded the gates and the way across –
'Fatty's scared to get too near.'

I'd watched them feather from wall to wall,
Powder tight-toed through creaking snow,
And I was last-
And lost in fear
Of the twelve-foot blackness of water below;

And the green-slimed cliffs and frozen hiss
Of the water whiskering from the gate,
And the dozen watchful, mocking eyes
Grinning with hate.

With all my courage left I ran,
Scrambled the bank and rolled the wire,
And from the lock their anger rose
And scorched my running like a fire.

Gregory Harrison

* What exactly is the child in the poem afraid of? Do you sympathise with him or her?

* Why do the others call out 'yaller'?

* How many ways can you find that they use to tease the child?

* How can they 'laugh like knives'?

* How can eyes 'grin with hate'?

* What happens in the last verse of the poem?

1. Write about what happens the next time the child meets the others. You may choose to write a poem or a story, and you may decide to look at what happens from the point of view of the child or as if you are one of the others.

* 'Sticks and stones
  May break my bones,
  But words will never hurt me.'
What do you think of this old saying?

* Have you ever been bullied? What did it feel like? What did you do about it?

* Have you ever bullied someone else? Can you remember why you did it?

* Are children or adults the worse bullies?

2. A friend of yours has been bullied or teased unkindly. Write about what happened as if you are telling the story years later.

John Polruddon

John Polruddon
All of a sudden
Went out of his house one night,

  When a *privateer*   *pirate-ship*
  Came sailing near
  Under his window-light.

They saw his jugs
His plates and mugs
His hearth as bright as brass,

  His *gews and gaws*   *valuable trinkets*
  And *kicks and shaws*   *and ornaments*
  All through their spying-glass.

They saw his wine
His silver shine
They heard his fiddlers play.

  'Tonight,' they said,
  'Out of his bed
  Polruddon we'll take away.'

And from a skiff
They climbed the cliff
And crossed the salt-wet lawn,

  And as they crept
  Polruddon slept
  The night away to dawn.

'In air or ground
What is that sound?'
Polruddon said, and stirred.

  They breathed, 'Be still,
  It was the shrill
  Of the scritch-owl you heard.'

'O yet again
I hear it plain,
But do I wake or dream?'

  'In morning's fog
  The otter-dog
  Is whistling by the stream.'

'Now from the sea

What comes for me
Beneath my window dark?'

   'Lie still, my dear,
   All that you hear
   Is the red-fox's bark.'

Swift from his bed
Polruddon was sped
Before the day was white,

   And head and feet
   Wrapped in a sheet
   They bore him down the height.

And never more
Through his own door
Polruddon went nor came,

   Though many a tide
   Has turned beside
   The cliff that bears his name.

On stone and brick
Was ivy thick,
And the grey roof was thin,

And winter's gale
With fists of hail
Broke all the windows in.

The chimney-crown
It tumbled down
And up grew the green,

   Till on the cliff
   It was as if
   A house had never been.

But when the moon
Swims late or soon
Across St Austell Bay,

   What sight, what sound
   Haunts air and ground
   Where once Polruddon lay?

It is the high
White scritch-owl's cry,
The fox as dark as blood,

   And on the hill
   The otter still
   Whistles beside the flood.

Charles Causley

This poem is about an incident that really occurred in Cornwall a long time ago.

* When you have read the poem yourself, move into groups of three or four and give one another the parts of story-teller, John Polruddon and the kidnappers. Then read the poem aloud several times. Read each part in different ways and try to agree on what you think is the best version.

1. Suppose that the disappearance had occurred recently.

Write the report which would appear on the front page of the local newspaper, recording the disappearance of John Polruddon, one of the wealthiest men in the town. Base your report on the facts which are given in the poem, but include, if you wish, maps, diagrams, illustrations and interviews with local people. Your report must include:

what	happened
when	it happened
how	it happened
where	it happened
who	was involved.

2. Radio and television reporters would obviously take an interest in the story.

Improvise radio or television interviews with John Polruddon's family and with servants in the house.

3. Suppose that, many years after the event, you are shown round the ruins of the house by a descendant of John Polruddon.

Write or improvise your conversation as this member of the Polruddon family explains, in answer to your questions, where each stage of the supposed kidnapping occurred, and what has happened to the house since then.

Spelling

here
where
there
nowhere

owl
fowl
howl
scowl

boat
coat
goat
throat

baked
braked
faked
raked

broken
spoken
token

fired
hired
tired

man   men
woman   women

seek
meek
A leek is a vegetable.
A week has seven days.

My shoe has a heel.
This pin is made of steel.
Here is a cotton reel.
Don't eat orange peel.

A beech tree grows slowly.
Say the speech softly.

I see with my eyes.

beak
peak
speak
The tank has a leak.
This tea is too weak.

The cut will heal.
A thief will steal.
It wasn't a ghost, it was real.
I hear the bells peal.

each
peach
reach
teach
The beach is rocky.

The sea is cold.

cry   cried
dry   dried
fry   fried
try   tried

catch
hatch
latch
match
satchel
snatch
watch

fetch

ditch
itch
pitch
witch

clutch
crutch
Dutch
hutch

drew
flew
grew
threw

could
would
should

bored
adored
scored
stored
restored

bony
slimy
grimy

hasty
tasty

calf	calves
half	halves
knife	knives
loaf	loaves
scarf	scarves
himself	themselves
shelf	shelves
wife	wives

awful
useful
wonderful
beautiful

eight
height
weight

lay	laid
pay	paid
say	said

a lot
all right
as well
in case
in fact

we're
you're
they're

remember
December
November
September

walk
talk

calm
palm
psalm

limb
climb

bomb
comb

crumb
dumb
numb
thumb

niece
piece
brief
chief
belief
relief

field

fiend
friend

fierce

achieve
believe
relieve

swab
swan
swap
swamp
swallow

guard
guarantee

guess
guessed

guest

kneel
knew

knife
knight
knit

knob
knock
knot

knuckle

famil**y**
familiar

carr**y**ing
marrying

worrying

hurrying

d**ie**t
quiet

our
your
their

appeared
applied
appointed
approached

act**or**
author
doctor
emperor
inventor
mayor
sailor

motor
tractor
elevator
escalator

baf**fle**
raffle

muffle
ruffle

fiddle
riddle

cuddle
muddle
puddle

muzzle
puzzle

fre**ckle**

prickle
tickle

happy   happiness
lazy   laziness
busy   business

diagon**al**
horizontal
vertical

diagonal**ly**
horizontally
vertically

s**our**
devour
The flour made good bread

pr**oud**
cloud
Shout aloud!

panic
pani**ck**ing

picnic
picni**ck**ing

con**fess**
confession
confessor

profess
profession
professor

gravel
travel

level
shovel

jewel
towel
trowel

winning
grinning
beginning

dinner
sinner
thinner
winner
beginner

dying
lying
trying
replying

decided
decision

wrap
wreck
wrist
write

science
conscience
conscientious
conscious

nervous
poisonous

neighbour
height
weight

ceiling
deceit
receipt

caught
taught
daughter
slaughter

lone
alone
lonely

lovely

barely
surely

probably
reasonably
reliably

Index to Language Topics

The authors and publishers wish to thank the following copyright owners for permission to quote from copyright works.

Page 9, from *Ginger Over the Wall* by Prudence Andrew, Lutterworth Press; page 11 reprinted by permission of the publisher from Nancy Rudolph, *Workyards* (New York: Teachers College Press, Copyright © 1974 by Teachers College, Columbia University. All rights reserved), pp 9–10; page 16 from *Adventure Playgrounds* by Jack Lambert and Jenny Pearson, Jonathan Cape Ltd; pages 18 and 164 from *Posting Letters* by Gregory Harrison, Oxford University Press; page 19 from *Hides and Seekers* by Harry T Sutton, Batsford; page 24 from *The Midnight Folk* by permission of The Society of Authors as the literary representative of the Estate of John Masefield; page 30 *They Saw it Happen 55 BC–1485*, Basil Blackwell Publisher; page 36, 'Suppose you met a Witch', © Ian Serraillier from *Belinda and the Swan*, Jonathan Cape Ltd; page 68 adapted from 'Thames Flood Defences', Greater London Council; page 72 from *Storm Surge* by David Rees, Lutterworth Press; page 79 from *The Kraken Wakes* by John Wyndham, Michael Joseph Ltd; page 84 from *The Bonny Pit Laddie* by Frederick Grice (1960), reprinted by permission of Oxford University Press; page 89 from *The Great Apple Raid* by Arthur Hopcroft, William Heinemann Ltd; page 91 'Hide and Seek' by Vernon Scannell; page 101 from *Animals and Friends and How to Keep Them* by Margaret Shaw and James Fisher, J M Dent and Sons Ltd; page 106 from *The Goalkeeper's Revenge* by Bill Naughton, Harrap; page 108 'The Meadow Mouse' reprinted by permission of Faber and Faber Ltd from *The Collected Poems of Theodore Roethke*; page 110 'Hedgehog' from *The Owl in the Tree* by Anthony Thwaite (1963). Reprinted by permission of Oxford University Press; pages 126 and 131 from *Folklore of Sussex* by Jacqueline Simpson, B T Batsford Ltd; page 134 'Welsh Incident' by Robert Graves from *Collected Poems*; page 137 from *Beowulf the Warrior* by Ian Serraillier (1964). Reprinted by permission of Oxford University Press; page 153 'Friends' from *As Large as Alone* by Elizabeth Jennings, Macmillan; page 155 from *Run for your Life* by David Line, Jonathan Cape Ltd; page 159 from *The Funny Guy* by Grace Hogarth, copyright © 1955 by Grace Hogarth, published by Penguin Books; page 162 from *My Mate Shofiq* by Jan Needler, Andre Deutsch Ltd; page 166 'John Polruddon' by Charles Causley from *Collected Poems 1951–1975*, Macmillan.

Photographs

Times Newspapers Ltd pages 7, 64; Barnaby's Picture Library pages 17, 40, 152, 153; Maurice Nimmo page 27; Popperfoto pages 66, 76, 129, 130; Avon Rubber Company Ltd page 78; Keystone Press page 83; Mary Evans Picture Library page 86; Mansell Collection page 86; Kunsthistorisches Museum, Vienna page 87; Frank W Lane pages 100, 109; Sue Chapman page 157; W Heath Robinson, *Inventions*, Duckworth page 151; Sven Oredsen page 161.